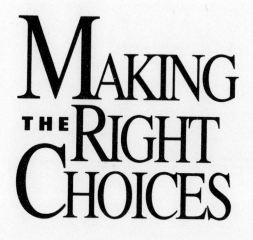

MAKING THE RIGHT CHOICES

MAKING THE RIGHT CHOICES

TED W. ENGSTROM
AND
NORMAN B. ROHRER

THOMAS NELSON PUBLISHERS
Nashville

Published in Nashville, Tennessee, by Thomas Nelson, Inc., Publishers, and distributed in Canada by Word Communications, Ltd., Richmond, British Columbia, and in the United Kingdom by Word (UK), Ltd., Milton Keynes, England.

Unless otherwise noted, Scripture quotations are from the NEW KING JAMES VERSION of the Bible. Copyright © 1979, 1980, 1982, Thomas Nelson, Inc., Publishers.

Scripture quotations noted KJV are from The Holy Bible, KING JAMES VERSION.

Scripture quotations noted NIV are taken from the HOLY BIBLE, NEW INTERNATIONAL VERSION ®. Copyright © 1973, 1978, 1984 by International Bible Society. Used by permission of Zondervan Bible Publishing House. All rights reserved.

The "NIV" and "New International Version" trademarks are registered in the United States Patent and Trademark Office by International Bible Society. Use of either trademark requires the permission of International Bible Society.

Scripture quotations noted RSV are from the REVISED STANDARD VERSION of the Bible. Copyright © 1946, 1952, 1971, 1973 by the Division of Christian Education of the National Council of the Churches of Christ in the U.S.A. Used by permission.

Scripture quotations noted TLB are from *The Living Bible* (Wheaton, Illinois: Tyndale House Publishers, 1971) and are used by permission.

Library of Congress Cataloging-in-Publication Data

Engstrom, Theodore Wilhelm, 1916—

   Making the right choices / Ted Engstrom and Norm Rohrer.

   p. cm.

   Includes bibliographical references.

   ISBN 0-8407-3510-3

   1. Men—Religious life.   2. Men—Conduct of life.
   3. Christian life—1060—   I. Rohrer, Norman B.   II. Title.
   BV4843.E64   1993
   248.8'42—dc20   93-1924
                                                    CIP

Printed in the United States of America
1 2 3 4 5 6 7 - 98 97 96 95 94 93

TO OUR SONS

CONTENTS

AUTHOR NOTE

We have collaborated in the writing of this book; however, from the start Ted Engstrom has been the key instigator for the project. We've therefore chosen to leave it in his voice, and any anecdotes introduced by an "I" are from him.

The struggle of men against moral indiscretion is as old as Cain and as new as tomorrow morning's newspaper. I have worked with men of many cultures around the world and their struggles are the same: to question God, to stray from commitment to their wives and children, to love money, to seek power, to vie for position, and to quit short of their goals.

Temptation most often does not rise up with reptilian horror. Usually it creeps subtly into a man's mind from the tempter. The Lord Jesus Christ faced Satan at the very beginning of the Savior's mission. Before He could preach a single message, before He could perform His first miracle, and before He could call others to follow Him—the way, the truth, and the life—out of the blue came the Serpent of the Garden of Eden. Satan appealed to the lust of the flesh, the lust of the eyes, and the pride of life at that vulnerable moment when the Lord was hungry and thirsty and alone. But our Lord showed that He would not be moved from the divine mandate.

Making the Right Choices offers direction for stouthearted men written by honorable Christian men whom I have known for many years. May its message strengthen fathers, sons, employers, and workmen in all areas of our society until they hear the Lord Jesus say, "Well done, good and faithful servant."

Ted W. Engstrom

WINNERS AND SINNERS

For more than seven decades and throughout three careers I have enjoyed friendships with a diverse fraternity of men. I have laughed with them and cried with them, hired them and fired them, battled them in sports and bowed with them in prayer, stood up for them at weddings and helped to dedicate their babies. And in decision-making crises I have profited by their wise counsel.

The distinctives of the men I have known vary greatly, of course. But I have learned that in the end there are only three types of men—those who have struggled against temptation and won, those who still struggle against it, and those who have been crushed by yielding to it. Let me give you some examples.

I think sometimes of a handsome young man in my college class who won the affection of a beautiful coed and married her after graduation. Before the age of thirty he had risen to a responsible position in a thriving company and was the envy of the other aspiring young leaders there. Slowly, however, he became a slave to alcohol. Eventually he lost his family, his career, and his friends because he could not beat his addiction.

Yet different was the experience of another of my schoolmates. This friend gladly gave up the chance to marry so he could dedicate himself to pioneering missionary work in the steaming jungles of the Amazon.

During my early years in the publishing business an older associate became a valuable mentor to me. He was the ideal of a man who worked hard, made sacrifices, and contributed sound judgment in executive decisions. Gradually, though, his long assignments away from his wife and children eroded his commitment to his wedding vows. He realized too late he had sought solace in the wrong places. Like the foolish young man of Proverbs 7:22, he went after a stranger "as an ox goeth to the slaughter, or as a fool to the correction of the stocks" (KJV). And in the process he lost those most precious to him.

A college president I know remembered his wedding vows years later when he made a decision to care for his wife beyond what might have been expected of him. When she fell victim to Alzheimer's disease, he resigned his position to give her his constant love and attention. He remained by her side, caring for her sanitation needs, feeding her, grooming her, changing her clothes, and reading to her, even though she was never able to respond to him during all those years, not even to indicate that she heard him or felt his abiding love.

I can never forget the man in my Sunday school class who scrimped and saved for years until he finally accumulated enough money to purchase a house for his wife and children. Yet just weeks before the family's move-in date, investigators at the bank where the man worked uncovered his clever but illegal maneuvering in financial dealings. Instead of enjoying his dream house, he was handcuffed and taken to prison. The contract for the house was canceled, and his loved ones were left without a provider.

Temptation often strikes when we least expect it. But one thing is certain: we *can* expect it.

A worker at a resort in the Sierra Mountains of California attached this bumper sticker to his pickup truck: "Lead Me Not Into Temptation, I Can Find It Myself." You know what he means. No one needs lessons in how to lure temptation. What men *do* need, rather, is the helping hand of a partner in prayer to resist temptation and overcome it. We need guidance, advice, and support from men who have lived long and have experienced much under the Lord's good hand.

Several years ago, I sat at a dinner party next to a sophisticated man of the world, a pagan if I ever knew one. He was extremely tense, so I sought to engage him in conversation. Before I knew it, my new friend was pouring out his troubles: His wife had grown cold and uncaring. His children didn't call him anymore. His blood pressure was too high. Competitors were cutting into his business market and lowering his income. Finally, he confided softly, "I'm tempted to do something I know I'll regret."

After listening to all this, I told him, "There is an answer to your problems."

He looked at me skeptically. "What's the answer?" he asked.

"The answer is to turn all of this over to God," I said.

His initial surprise and annoyance gradually gave way to curious interest. In the course of the conversation I obtained his business card, and later wrote to him and included a letter in a small package of books. He must have read them all, because soon I received a glowing response from him. "I did it!" he exclaimed. "I knelt down in my home and surrendered my life to Jesus Christ. It was the answer just as you said."

He and his wife fell in love again. New lines of communication opened up with his children. And his restless pursuit of power and wealth were replaced with goals to follow the humble, lowly Nazarene.

It doesn't matter whether you are a student in junior high school, a businessman in corporate headquarters, a researcher in the jungles of Africa, or a man of eighty-five living alone and nearing the end of his life. *Whoever you are, you can never escape temptation.* Temptation is the gate that leads to cheating, lying, gossiping, sexual impurity, and all kinds of sins.

I have seen temptation rise up like a hideous reptile with eyes blazing and present itself with sweet reasonableness and ample justification. Yet good motives for a sin don't make it any less a sin. Neither do excuses:

- "It's not my fault. I was only protecting myself."
- "You can't blame me. My parents neglected me. They're the ones to blame."
- "Too bad, that's just the way I am. God gave me appetites, and I'm only doing what comes naturally."
- "It's every man for himself out there. I'm only trying to survive."

You can't analyze temptation logically or figure it out mathematically. I know from experience that not every temptation falls into a neat, well-defined category. Each lure to sin has its own intrigue. Some men go to jail for yielding to temptation, but most hide their shortcomings and pay the price in lost friendships, broken homes, frustrating employment, or mental anguish.

Yet men who overcome their temptations can make a powerful impact on society. Consider my friend Roy. Every weekday, a carpool van carries Roy and five other engineers up Freeway 57 from the city of Orange, California to their office in San Bernardino and then home again at night. One morning one of the engineers, a Muslim from Nigeria, turned to my Christian brother and said, "Roy, I can tell you're a man who has wrestled with temptation and beaten it."

Roy thought for a moment and replied, "You're right. I have wrestled with temptation, and now I'm on the winning side." The Muslim must have thought much about this while at work that day, because during the return trip home that night he asked Roy if he was a Christian.

Would your associates know you are a Christian by the way you handle temptation? Or are you on the verge of doing something you will later regret? Are you fulfilled in your family, at work, with fellow believers at church, and in your private time with God? If not, I cordially invite you to partake of the abundant supply of battle rations provided by men who have been in situations like yours and are eager to share what they have learned.

Why comes temptation, but for man to meet
And master and make crouch beneath his foot,
And so be pedestaled in triumph?
—Robert Browning, *The Ring and the Book*

A^{TO}BDICATE

Satan o'ercomes none,
but by willingness.
—Robert Henrick[1]

ONE _____

_____

A generation ago Richard Rodgers and Oscar Hammerstein introduced the thrilling refrains of the now-classic musical number, "Stouthearted Men." They effused in the lyrics that if they had a few stouthearted men they would, in short order, be able to count ten-thousand in the ranks. Under orders we would all march shoulder to shoulder until all of us accepted our leadership roles. We were going to make families happy, safe, and secure with dad as their head. Leaders in finance, government, and the Church were going to give masculine luster to a secure society, from the sweet cradle of innocence unto the yellow leaf when

> The flowers and fruits of Love are gone;
> The worm, the canker, and the grief
> Are mine alone! [2]

No one questioned the nobility and values of such goals years ago when "Stouthearted Men" first played. So I ask you today: What strange compulsion causes a man to deceive, defraud, abuse, delude, mislead, bilk, fleece, and deliberately set aside his morals for passing pleasures when such lofty opportunities are his? Why would a man yield to a fleeting sexual temptation and shatter a trusting, loving relationship with his wife that took years to build? What man would lie to make a sale, knowing that as he does so he builds his future on quicksand? How could a man expect to rise to a position of authority by misrepresenting himself? Where could he hide if he refused to accept his responsibility for the welfare of his family, himself, and all who look to him for leadership?

Men, you can *expect* to be tempted to put work ahead of family, abuse time, steal, cheat, waste talents, elevate sports above everything else, let things slide, be lazy, eat too much, drink too much, and make excuses for it all.

Pray this prayer with me: "When there is opportunity, take away my inclination. When there is inclination, take away my opportunity."

In 1988, sixty years after Rodgers and Hammerstein wrote "Stouthearted Men," the *Boston Globe* carried this story: "Wanted: Some Stouthearted Men." The article began, "What's wrong with America?" The author quickly answered his own question: "Lousy leadership. Not just in government or politics, but in business and labor, service and manufacturing, education and other institutions, and the media, too."[3]

The Master and Temptation

If you want to know how to handle temptation, then learn from the greatest man who ever lived. At age thirty our Lord was preparing to begin the mission for which He had come, and He didn't have to wait long for temptation to raise its ugly head. Before He could preach His first message, perform His first miracle, and call others to follow Him, out of the blue the tempter struck.

The devil searched for a chink in Jesus' divine armor, hoping for compromise. He watched for areas of weakness in Him at a vulnerable time by appealing to the lust of the flesh, the lust of the eyes, and the pride of life. But Jesus showed He would not be moved from His divine mandate.

How easy it would have been for Him to succumb to the temptation to accept bread after forty days without food; to enjoy instant prestige by leaping off the mountain and having angels rescue Him in a dramatic display of protective power; to take the high road of sensationalism to the throne, while leaving in their sins those He had come to save. But Christ prevailed against the temptation. And by His grace, so can you. He calls to men today, "Follow me."

We Are Hit Where We Are Strong

Jesus' temptation by the devil in the wilderness exposes the false notion that we are tempted in our areas of weakness. The opposite is true. We men are tempted in the areas of our strengths: A man gifted with charisma will be tempted to use his charm to get whatever he wants. A man gifted with eloquence will be tempted to talk his way out of misconduct. A brilliant man will be tempted to exploit his intellectual prowess for selfish reasons. Indeed, temptation strikes first where we are strongest, so we must be forever alert.

Many prominent men have let down their guard. In the midst of their greatest strengths came Watergate, Irangate, Pearlygate, the Keating savings-and-loan debacle, and other scandals. New missteps seem to surface daily. Add to these the moral weaknesses of prominent congressmen who perjure themselves and embellish past academic and military records. The military records alone of recent political candidates provide enough information to argue for weaknesses in the moral character of our leaders.

I chuckled when I read of a prayer by the chaplain of the Kansas Senate, Fred Holloman. He implored the Lord:

> Omniscient Father:
> Help us to know who is telling
> the truth. One side tells us one
> thing, and the other just the opposite.
> And if neither side is telling the truth,
> we would like to know that, too. [4]

Walking a Fine Line

Most men hide their temptations on life's journey. They rein in their emotions and stick to a rigid logic about life. Their wives, business associates, and fishing buddies aren't always sure what they are feeling. Sometimes men aren't sure either.

A man today struggles with contradictory expectations. As a youngster he is considered "all boy" if he is active, boisterous, and playful. Yet as a man he is often expected to sit for long stretches, working passively at a tedious job when he feels like doing anything *other* than what he is doing at the moment.

A boy may be encouraged to take risks, be brave, and exert his masculinity in innocent games. Yet as a man he may be laughed at for not accepting a challenge, even though his reasoning tells him defeat is certain. A man is usually required to be aggressive and achievement-oriented in his career. Yet at home he must switch gears completely and become tender and emotionally integrated. If a father becomes involved in caring for his baby, he risks clashing with his wife over child-raising roles. Yet if he pulls back too far, staying out of the picture and trying not to interfere, he risks being seen as passive, uninvolved, and weak.

A man is never supposed to complain. He is expected to fix things, to set wrong things right. Yet he cannot afford to be emotionally distant from his loved ones and friends.

Needless to say, men risk suffering split personalities, doing none of their jobs well. They have a fine line to walk.

To Tell the Truth

A recent survey of 2,000 Americans undertaken by two advertising executives asked questions about love, marriage, work, leisure, religion, and commitment to the morals upon which this nation was built. The results of that survey by Jim Patterson and Peter Kim are presented in their book, *The Day America Told the Truth*—and they are anything but encouraging. "Yesterday's verities have vanished," they write. "Unpredictability and chaos have become the norm."[5] Perhaps most discouraging of all is that whatever tragic conclusions the surveys showed of women went double for men. Here is a sampling of answers from male respondents:

- I don't see the point in observing the Sabbath (77 percent).
- I will steal from those who won't really miss it (74 percent).
- I will lie when it suits me, so long as it doesn't cause any real damage (64 percent).
- I will drink and drive if I feel that I can handle it. I know my limit (56 percent).
- I will cheat on my spouse—after all, given the chance, he or she will do the same (53 percent).
- I will procrastinate at work and do absolutely nothing about one full day in every five. It's standard operating procedure (50 percent).
- I will use recreational drugs (41 percent).
- I will cheat on my taxes—to a point (30 percent).

- I will put my lover at risk of disease. I sleep around a bit, but who doesn't? (31 percent).
- Technically, I may have committed date rape, but I know that she wanted it (20 percent have committed date rape).[6]

Such attitudes can be excused by calling them "situation ethics," but Dietrich Bonhoeffer took another view of the matter. Shortly before he was executed by his Nazi persecutors, he eloquently addressed the issue of the temptations we face: "Believers all wear the flesh which in Jesus Christ conquered Satan. Because Satan cannot bring down the fall of the Son of God, he pursues him now with all temptations in his members."[7]

The authors of *The Day America Told the Truth* lay the bulk of blame for a decline in morality with men:

Our current ethics at work are low, but they'd be a lot lower were it not for the great number of women who've entered the work force in recent years.

When we compared the answers given by the two sexes, we confirmed that women in this country simply behave more ethically than men.

On every question we probed, American women in the workplace held to a higher moral standard than men did. . . .

Less than half as many women as men believe that the only way to get ahead is to cheat, and not as many believe in politics rather than work as the way to success. . . .

In addition, women are much less willing to compromise their values to get ahead and somewhat more willing to quit as a matter of principle if they learn that their company is engaging in illegal activities. . . .

If valuable company property is stolen, the thief will be a man six times in seven.[8]

Christians in Deeds

The saddest news of all, however, is that statistically there is little difference between the ethical opinions and practices of the religious man and the nonreligious man. Doug Sherman and William Hendricks, in their book *Keeping Your Ethical Edge Sharp,* cite a Gallup poll showing that 37 percent of people who attend church admit to pilfering work supplies, compared to 43 percent of those who don't attend church. Thirteen percent of the churchgoers use the company phone for long-distance personal calls, compared to 17 percent of those who don't attend.[9]

Is this really true of genuine believers? Yes, say Sherman and Hendricks. The ethical conduct of Christians varies only slightly from that of non-Christians. Christians are nearly as likely as unbelievers to cheat on their income tax forms, copy from other students on tests, pay money under the table to building contractors, disregard legal specifications during construction, copy a computer program without paying for it, make unreported calls on the company telephone, misrepresent a product to make a sale, and obey only the laws that are convenient for them.

I Sought for a Man . . ."

Long ago the word of the Lord came to the prophet Ezekiel saying,

The people of the land have used oppressions, committed robbery, and mistreated the poor and needy; and they wrongfully oppress the stranger. So I sought for a man among them who would make a wall, and stand in the gap before Me on behalf of the land, that I should not destroy it; but I found no one.
(Ezek. 22:29–30)

Even a casual observer of such a scene must conclude that the moral bankruptcy of Ezekiel's day is characteristic of America today. Our leaders give advice, but few heed it. "If everybody's breaking the rules," many reason, "am I a complete fool to play by them myself?"

Many of us men hide large portions of our lives from our closest friends. Too often we say things we don't mean, socialize with people we don't like, and fail to stand up for what we believe. A majority of us can't go through a week without lying. And instead of striving to become better *men*, we give lavish attention to losing weight and making our body, hair, and face more attractive.

Is all of this new? Hardly. The Apostle Paul describes the universality of man's depravity in Romans 3: "Their throat is an open tomb; / With their tongues they have practiced deceit; / The poison of asps is under their lips" (verse 13). Even after we men are converted, we often waffle about the truth unless we daily place ourselves under the lordship of Christ and struggle hard to stay there.

Before a New York writer wrote a bestselling novel he said he hadn't bothered with fiction because what was reported in the news every day was more interesting and shocking than anything he could make up.

Unfortunately, the flow of daily news seems to back him up. More and more men frankly admit to illicit affairs. Even pastors and other Christian leaders are being forced to confess that they have broken ranks with the faithful and have fallen into the very sins against which they've preached. They usually stay with their wives while their affairs continue.

Women have described men—sometimes accurately—as predators, bullies, the primary provider, even as meal tickets. Most women express some fear about the violent side of American men. Many wonder or worry whether a man can be sensitive and yet not be a wimp. These attitudes remain consistent in both rural and urban parts of the country.

America's saddest "secret," however, is the abused children who grow up to become troubled adults likely to pass along their suffering to their children. One in six adults across America reports having been physically abused during childhood. Almost as many—one in seven—confess that they were victims of sexual abuse as children. Four in ten Americans know someone who was abused as a child.[10] Bear in mind that most people who were abused as children never tell anyone.

Amid the horrors of a society that is in moral shambles, calls out for godly people to "Watch, stand fast in the faith, be brave, be strong" (1 Cor. 16:13). Men, we must resist the temptation to let someone else fight against suicide, government corruption, child abuse, infidelity, drug abuse, violence, and rape.

Charles R. Swindoll cites three practical exhortations to remember when temptation presents itself:

Expect it. Don't be alarmed by it. You will never know a level of peace that gives you a thick envelope or bubble of untouchable security.

Detect it. Call it what it is. The adversary has numerous plans of attack, and they are seldom overt. He is insidious, brilliant, and clever, and knows the exact place where he can grab your attention.

Reject it. I find younger Christians rolling up their spiritual sleeves and saying, "Come on, devil. I'll take you on." There is great danger in that. If you try to play clever games with the enemy you will lose. He'll whip you ever time. Say no! [11]

Jesus holds out a way of escape to each man who is tempted, just as He did to Judas Iscariot at the Last Supper. Walter Wangerin, Jr., provides a poignant glimpse of what happened in that historic moment. When the Lord knew the awful temptation facing Judas and saw His betrayal coming, He took steps to stop it by giving the disciple three distinct gifts:

1. *Knowledge.* Judas must now know the moral quality and the consequence of the deed. It is betrayal. Betrayal is wrong.
2. *Free will.* Knowledge frees Judas from ignorance *and* from the compulsive quality of the act. Now he can and must choose.
3. *Sole responsibility.* If he proceeds on his course after all, he alone shall own the deed.[12]

The Lord had indeed set His face toward the Cross, but, no, Judas did not have to betray Him. *Jesus had given him a choice!* The disciple could have shouted, "Yes! It is I who am your betrayer! Forgive me, Lord!" He could have embraced the offer and stopped. But, instead, the temptation of money overcame him—and he stumbled blindly onward and wrecked his life.

Men, the glitter of our society continues to tempt us relentlessly with the serpent's lure. Be aware of its obsessions and pornotopias, for too many in our ranks have fallen already. Put disciplined hedges around your life. Be real about your sexuality and do not cry smugly, "I could never do such a thing!"

Fill your mind with God's Word. Pray. Be accountable to a friend for your actions. Choose the narrow path. The reward for these disciplines is no less than abundant life on earth and unspeakable joys with our Lord for eternity.

> *No temptation has overtaken you except such as is common to man; but God is faithful, who will not allow you to be tempted beyond what you are able, but with the temptation will also make the way of escape, that you may be able to bear it.*
> *—1 Corinthians 10:13*

P TO BE ROMISCUOUS

Lust is the ape that gibbers in our loins. Tame
him as we will by day, he rages all the wilder
in our dreams by night. Just when we think
we're safe from him, he raises up his ugly head
and smirks, and there's no river in the world
flows cold and strong enough to strike him
down. Almighty God, why dost thou deck
men out with such a loathsome toy?
—Frederick Buechner[1]

TWO

I doubt anyone could name an element that has shaken society as drastically as have a man's hormones. What was God's idea with this phenomenon, anyway? Why weren't men fashioned more like animals, who go about life with hardly a thought toward sex except during certain seasons?

Lust keeps the hungry presses churning out pornographic literature. It fattens lawyers' wallets in divorce courts. Lust destroys careers, initiates fights, shatters dreams, fosters distrust, spreads disease, and sends many of its young victims to an early grave. Some irreverently call sexual passion "God's mistake," and place it in the same category as natural disasters like tornadoes and earthquakes.

At the beginning of the Communist revolution, Marxists set out to correct "God's mistake." Lenin included sex among the human traits that needed to be altered. To him, this human appetite had no more meaning than the quenching of thirst by a glass of water. He hoped that "bourgeois morality" would crumble along with its financial institutions, its industries, and its religion.

Yet, as it turned out, sex was immune to reductionist logic. It refused to lie down and behave.

Lenin, a historian, should have known better—after all, kings had renounced their thrones for sex, saints had recanted their faith for it, and spouses had left their lifetime mates to pursue the strange hunger called lust. What chance did dialectic materialism have to change it?

God never caused any person to lust, of course. Each is tempted "when he is drawn away by his own desires and enticed" (James 1:14). Sin has done terrible things to us men, and among the worst is a confusion of values. Only with God's gracious intervention can we determine what is good for us, for sexual excitement can blaze up in a man's bosom a hundred times a day.

"Pornotopia"

It is hard to make any sense of the Niagara of shameful programming pouring into the homes of America through television. It's in advertising, TV programs themselves, and even in the news. Titillating sensuality washes over us daily, continually pushing prurient desires upon younger and younger audiences.

Fortunately, federal laws force television networks to omit sexually explicit programming until after midnight. However, cable companies are exempt from this law, so the barn door is left wide open. Professor David A. J. Richard of New York University Law School numbers himself among those who advocate increased freedom for hard-core pornography. He calls it "a 'pornotopia'—a view of sensual delight in the erotic celebration of the body, a concept of easy freedom without consequences, a fantasy of timeless repetitive indulgence."[2]

Men in the Church are feeling the heat of this so-called "freedom," and many have succumbed to sexual temptation. In 1988 *Leadership* magazine published a poll of one thousand pastors. Some 12 percent said they had committed adultery while in the ministry—that's one out of eight pastors! Twenty-three percent stated they had done things that were sexually inappropriate.[3]

Leadership Magazine polled a thousand of its subscribers who were *not* pastors and discovered that the figure was nearly double: 23 percent had had extramarital intercourse, and 45 percent had done something they considered to be sexually inappropriate. One in four Christian men has been unfaithful, and nearly one-half have behaved unbecomingly.[4]

Dr. R. Kent Hughes, senior pastor of College Church in Wheaton, Illinois, offers this opinion:

"This leads us to an inescapable conclusion: The contemporary evangelical Church, broadly considered, is 'Corinthian' to the core. It is being stewed in the molten juices of its own sensuality so . . . "

- No wonder the Church has lost its grip on holiness.
- No wonder it is so slow to discipline its members.
- No wonder it is dismissed by the world as irrelevant.
- No wonder so many of its children reject it.
- No wonder it has lost its power in many places—and that Islam and other false religions are making so many converts.[5]

"We walk in a world of shadow," wrote A. W. Tozer, "where real things appear unreal and things of no consequence are sought after as eagerly as if they were made of the very gold that paves the streets of the City of God. . . . Moral astigmatism throws everything out of focus."[6]

I thought of Tozer's "moral astigmatism" as I read an article entitled "The War Within" in a 1982 issue of *Leadership*. The article contained the confessions of a young Christian leader who had fallen into the trap of sexual addiction.

One night while on a speaking mission, the young married pastor checked into a hotel room far from home where he surprised himself by making his first willful commitment to lust. As he paged through the city's entertainment guide, he kept flipping back to photographs of an exotic dancer, a nightclub feature in a hotel not far away.

At first, the minister instinctively ruled her show out of bounds. But as he settled down to watch TV, "Miss Exotic" kept appearing in his imagination. Soon the simple question "Why not?" had to be answered. Like the "young man devoid of understanding" so eloquently described in Proverbs 7, the minister was soon out the door and headed toward the nightclub. He awkwardly ordered a drink, something he had never done before, and soon was sipping his first whiskey and watching "Miss Exotic" cavort in scanty togs.

> With her enticing speech she
> caused him to yield,
> With her flattering lips she
> seduced him.
> (Prov. 7:21)

There followed in this man's life an odyssey of unleashed passion that he felt powerless to control. Back home he built a secret stash of pornographic magazines. After a morning of sermon preparation, he often "rewarded" himself with a look at photographs of nude women featured in the latest copy of *Oui* or *Playboy*. He continued to patronize sex clubs to watch nude dancers, became a voyeur and a self-stimulator.

Locked into his passions, this pastor began to rationalize his lust as follows:

> Nudity is art. Go to any art museum in the world, and you will see nudity openly displayed. The

human form is beautiful, and it would be puritanical to cut off appreciation for it. *Playboy* is photographed well, with an aesthetic, not prurient tone.

Playboy and its kin have great articles. There's the Jimmy Carter interview, for example, and *Penthouse's* conversation with Jerry Falwell. I must keep up with such material.

Some stimulation will help my sex life. I have a problem approaching my wife and communicating my desire for sex to her. I need a sort of boost, a stimulant to push me to declare my intentions.

Other people do far worse. I know many Christian leaders who still do all the things I toyed with, and worse. For that matter, look at Bible characters—as randy a bunch as you'll ever meet. There's probably no such thing as a pure person anyway; everybody has some outlet.

What is lust anyhow, I kept asking myself. Is fantasizing wrong in itself? If so, then erotic dreams would count as sin, and how could I be responsible for my dreams? I reminded myself of the definition of lust I had started with long before: desiring intercourse with a specific sexual partner. I experience a general sexual heightening, a raising of the voltage, not a specific desire for the act of intercourse.[7]

The pastor justified his actions in a perverse way by reminding himself that Augustine had prayed as a young man: "Give me chastity, but not yet." Before becoming a Roman monk, Augustine sampled every sensual delight and withheld nothing from his imagination and his actions. The irony for the pastor was that he began to "hate sex" with his wife. The pleasure it was designed to provide actually waned in his experience. Soon he began to imagine himself "pure and godly" if only he could put sexual passion out of his life.

Slowly this sexual neurotic experienced deliverance from the fantasies that had shackled him for a decade. He came to see that, after all, the sweet-looking woman with an alluring smile who let a customer see her nude body would not give him the time of day if she sat next to him on an airplane! The turning point came for him following a successful spiritual life conference in New Hampshire. He was spending the night with a dear friend who at that time was pastor of one of the largest churches in the South, and soon the young man found himself confessing everything. His friend sat for a long time with a sad countenance. Finally his lip began to quiver, his face twitched, and his eyes filled with tears. Suddenly he began to sob—"great, huge, wretched sobs such as I had seen only at funerals."

After a few minutes the truth erupted. His friend was sobbing because of his own terrible addiction to lust! He had been taking pills for the venereal disease and anal infections he had contracted. Every horrible detail of the pastor's deviance came pouring out that night, including the divorce litigation that had ended his marriage. The irony was that this man was held in great esteem by Christian leaders and the laity. "His insights, compassion, and love were all more mature than mine," the young pastor wrote. "My sermons were like freshman practice runs compared to his. He was a godly man if I had ever met one, but underneath all that. . . . My inner fear jumped uncontrollably. I sensed the power of evil."[8]

It took ten years for this young man's prayers to be answered. Eventually, in a way he had never known before, he had an experience with God, the depth and intimacy of which stunned him. Now passion has returned to his marriage. His wife, loving and forgiving, is again the object of his affections. "*Her* body, no one else's, is gradually gaining the gravitational pull that used to be scattered in the universe of sexes. The act of sex, as often a source of irritation and trauma for me as an experience of pleasure, is beginning to take on the form of mystery and transcendence and inexpressible delight that its original design must have called for."9

The lingering remnants of grace in the city of man, the restored minister concluded, sometimes bear a striking resemblance to what awaits us in the City of God.

I have never known the horror of standing before a church, a board of directors, my wife and children, or friends and acquaintances to confess an illicit affair. But I have listened with sadness in my heart to the confessions of others. It is a sad moment for everyone whom adultery touches. I believe Satan has little interest in killing a man of God who is a trophy of grace. Instead, he rests neither day nor night to devise hidden snares to trip him up and then parade him in the chains of disgrace and shame. A minister's fall impacts society scandalously, but any Christian's fall diminishes the cause of Christ.

It is wholesome and godly to fear disqualification. We need friends to hold our feet to the fire, to point out our areas of weakness, to keep pride away, and to provoke us to cry out to God for His power and victory.

The Army taught us what to do quickly when we captured a hill. That was the time to set up a hasty defense, arrange a network of communication, and set boundaries beyond which the enemy could not pass. The moment of victory was no time to relax, count blessings, or take a coffee break. The same holds true in spiritual warfare. A man must live his Christian life with a hasty defense always in place. And we live in a time when every Christian must earn daily the right to be respected.

When Leaders Falter

The *lapsus calami* of yesterday's spiritual leaders are chronicled in dusty books. The improprieties of today's shepherds, however, are more likely to be splashed across the tabloids at supermarket checkout counters. Jim Bakker, the founder of one of America's most publicized television ministries, *The PTL Club*, went to jail for illegal financial procedures in one of the most widely reported scandals in Christendom.

During Jim Bakker's trial and later imprisonment, his wife, Tammy Faye, bravely stood by her husband. She defended him on the nightly news and held together their tiny ministry in Orlando. Later, just as it appeared that perhaps PTL's troubles were fading from the news, photographs of the Bakkers returned to the tabloids because Tammy had decided to divorce her husband three years before he was eligible for parole. "I still love the Lord with all of my heart," Tammy stated strangely in a letter to her constituents. "God's calling is still a fire that burns within me."[10]

Before the scandal broke, while the *Charlotte Observer* was investigating Heritage U.S.A., the Bakkers had cried, "Enough is enough!" *Men, the same charge should be made against those who reject biblical standards of moral purity and ethical conduct and yet expect to continue in ministry.* How many people will stumble over the willful, sexual sins of a pastor or evangelist who sins and yet continues undeterred as head of his congregation and global ministry? What more will it take to force trusted shepherds to remain on the path to the Celestial City and avoid detours to the sloughs of despond?

The young minister who wrote "The War Within" in *Leadership* testified that he was set free from his obsessions. Guilt and fear forced him to face his sin and led him to repentance.

Counselors today, both Christian and secular, often mistakenly deal with the guilt and fear their clients experience rather than the cause of that guilt and fear which most often is sin. When former

President Ronald Reagan asked that sexual abstinence be taught as the best option for young people who wish to avoid the health dangers of promiscuity, detractors objected to the idea as a "guilt trip" and "scare tactics."

Yet even some Christians wonder why we're so uptight about sex. "Why not loosen up a little?" they ask. "Human sexuality is a gift from God." That casual attitude has resulted in a startling statistic. Research shows that of Christian households which have cable televison, 23 percent subscribe to pornography channels—the same percentage as the nation as a whole![11]

Many men are puzzled by human sexuality. In some ways theirs does resemble animal appetites and behavior. But the nature of sexuality is intended not merely for procreation but also as an expression of relationship. Animals perform sexual acts in the open; human beings insist on privacy. Mark Twain once observed, "Man is the only animal that blushes, or needs to."[12]

For the godly man, sex is different. He is not frustrated by it. Rather, it holds an aura of mystery—of holiness and of beauty. It enhances a man's love for his wife, builds strong ties between them, and yields the blessing of offspring and the heritage of a healthy family.

All of this is missing between homosexual lovers. In 1970, the Kinsey Institute published reports showing that 40 percent of white male homosexuals in San Francisco had had at least 500 sexual partners, and that 28 percent reported having had more than 1,000 partners.[13] Today, fear of AIDS has greatly reduced the number of such encounters, and the lie of "safe sex" is absurdly trusted to provide pleasure without risk.

In Training for Godliness

Men, we are in this world on a sacred mission. How can we who are called to lead and heal ever take advantage of our power to destroy? Yet in experiences of human lust, our gender stands out as the dominant offender. Men have on record far more instances of sexual misconduct than women. They buy pornographic literature that women find repulsive.

Detours into pornography offer only illusion and emptiness, but fidelity to one's wife offers enormous rewards in all areas of life. The guarded life of holiness is never easy, however. We will find fulfillment only by living up to the demands of the Creator, and He is not silent on these matters. "How can a young man keep his way pure?" asks the psalmist. "By living according to your word" (Ps. 119:9 NIV). I know a young man whose memorization of 1 Thessalonians 4:3-8 kept him pure. He hid in his heart such passages as Job 31:1, Proverbs 5 and 6:25-26, Mark 9:43-48, Ephesians 5:3-7, and 2 Timothy 2:22. These contributed to his stability and rewarded him with a happy home, a contented wife, children who are in subjection to the Lord, and respect and advancement in his employment. No amount of sensual lust can come close to the joys that such discipline brings.

Single Men and Their Temptations

Apart from hunger and sleep, the most powerful of all human urges and drives is the sexual appetite. Christians have the same biochemical forces working within their bodies as do nonbelievers who burn with erotic passion. Most of us want to be married, but the apostle Paul challenged us to seek not to be married, but instead to give ourselves to the work of God without distraction (1 Cor. 7:26). If a young man or woman can stay single and be morally pure, that person's reward will be great in heaven.

Men remain or become single for many reasons: the death of a spouse, divorce, a desire for freedom, to make time for a cause, dedication to a career, neurotic fear of intimacy, unrealistic expectations of the opposite sex, and perhaps unattractive physical and psychological traits to a prospective mate. A single life is not a disaster or a tragedy; many single men live full, rich, rewarding lives. They are able to have deep, gratifying friendships. It is generally thought that persons who are happily married would have been happily single as well.

Many men who are shy around the opposite sex see women as powerful, desirable, necessary, and rejecting. A healthy relationship consists of mutual giving and taking; a healthy couple works to meet each other's needs. But many shy singles cannot tolerate such an arrangement. Often unconsciously, they demand that the opposite sex fulfill their wishes, yet they themselves are able to fulfill few needs of others. Such people deal with the opposite sex on a narrow, limited basis. They greet any aggression or independence with hurt feelings or withdrawal. The lover of such an immature person feels smothered, trapped, and restricted.

Rick, a neighbor of one of our sons, for example, was by all appearances a wonderful specimen of manhood. He might have been chosen to play Prince Charming in the neighborhood theater. Always courteous and polite, he treated women as china dolls. "Yes, ma'am," and "No, ma'am," were his consistent responses to women, even to those his own age.

Rick did not assert himself. His dates always had to decide where they would go. A young woman's hopes for romance with him soon turned to disappointment because she quickly realized he crumbled whenever she showed strength.

What was behind this courteous marshmallow's behavior? *Rick's temptation was to view all women as he did his mother: as being perfect.* Yet to hold to this viewpoint, he had to deny a lot of obvious data to the contrary.

Why did Rick need to keep his mother flawless? He believed the obvious lie to avoid facing any negative feelings about her. He feared that he would no longer be worthy of his mother's love; therefore he kept his aggression shackled. To keep himself from feeling angry, then, he had to see other women as perfect.

As a child, when Rick allowed himself to express anger, his mother either ignored him or strongly disapproved. She was an intense woman who couldn't handle her own emotions well. Rick learned early: *I can't let myself be free because Mother will get mad.*

Today Rick has worked through many of his fears and fantasies. He realizes he can be strong and still be loved. He has been willing to give up a fantasy that he is a little boy and that every female must be a mother figure. By changing his perspectives and dealing with his fantasies, Rick has been able to relate to females in a more relaxed and natural manner. Now he allows himself to be genuine without his former inhibitions taking over.

The Temptation to Be Perfect

A friend of mine—we'll call him David—was a college student in his mid-twenties who clung to the temptation that he could be perfect. Outwardly he was unusually composed. His hair was well styled and he dressed impeccably. He was always precise in his choice of colors and fabrics. Everything about him seemed perfect.

His professors pegged him as the ideal student, yet his friends suspected he was quite disturbed. When

I knew David, he was headed for the ministry. But a therapist friend of mine told me not to be surprised if David was arrested someday as a child molester because of his obsession for denying his compulsions, and presenting himself as someone he wasn't.

The Temptation to Cling to Mother

A young man involved in a ministry in which I once worked had a mother who was strong and possessive. "Brian" was her only child, and he became the focus of her entire life. When Brian showed signs of independence, his mother would seductively win him back. He soon learned that if he was going to be loved by his mother, he would have to quench his aggression and put aside any thoughts of independence. He felt her love only when he remained dependent, nonaggressive, and "sweet."

Yet Brian felt strong only when he became angry. During his adolescent years he and his mother fought often, but Brian could never break her tie to him. As a result he became syrupy sweet and indecisive. Females pegged him as "Mr. Milquetoast." But now Brian is breaking free from his mother. He too is learning to assert himself. One day he will be a sensitive person with a good balance between tenderness and assertiveness.

Men, I know that unfulfilled sexual desires can be tormenting—the troubled mind, the confused emotions, the spiritual suffering one can experience. You may sometimes think your desires are too attractive to pass up. But keep in mind, you who are unmarried: *The anguish of the temptation is nothing compared with the suffering that results from the consequences of sin.* There are tears, remorse, possible disease, shattered relationships, unwanted children. The clock only moves forward, and no amount of repenting or apologizing can change what has happened.

Married Men and Temptation

Marriage is a painting, not a photograph. Watch as a master artist strokes his brush on a blank canvas: His first splash of color is bright orange down the middle. Next he dabs a blob of green in the extreme righthand corner. *Surely he must be practicing!* you think. His next stroke is a black, oval figure in the middle. Finally, as the painting emerges under the stroke of his skillful hand, a landscape begins to take shape. The orange slash becomes a stately tree, the green blob develops into hills in the background, and the dark oval is finally a blue pond which becomes the focus of our attention. The final scene is breathtakingly beautiful, and the viewer quickly forgets that such beauty was missing in the early stages of filling the blank canvas.

Many men wrongly view marriage as a photograph instead of a painting. They imagine the wedding ceremony as the finalization of their growing up, rather than a continuation of it. They do not realize that part of being a man means certain changes in one's personality. (Some of those changes are radical!) A man's personality is not set in concrete by the time of his marriage ceremony. Many men experience the greatest changes of their lives after their thirties. As we grow, we change our perspectives of ourselves and others. The relationship a man has with his wife the day he is married cannot possibly be maintained, nor is it meant to be.

A man who was raised in the Northwest discovered this almost too late. Henry was a philosophy major. He spent hours reading the philosophers, from Socrates to Sartre. The world of ideas fascinated him. He had little tolerance for people with more practical minds. He began to date Doris, who appreciated his ideas and admired his intellect and his facile use of six-syllable words. Part of his gratification in dating Doris was hearing her adoring comments on his intellect.

Eventually they married, but Henry knew he couldn't support his family by reciting philosophy. So he acquired a teaching position, which involved relating to people. But not everyone Henry worked with was as enthusiastic about his philosophy as was his wife. And even she occasionally yearned to discuss the mundane.

Marriage is a struggle not only with words. It involves flesh against flesh, will against will. And Henry was less adept in these struggles than in the world of ideas. Love is the final product. Love is having the profound desire for the other person's maximum development and gratification. Love is doing as much as possible for the pleasure of the *other person*. And to do the most loving thing takes a good deal of reasoning, judgment, and prayer.

I like what Edwin Louis Cole, head of Christian Men's Network, says in his book *On Becoming a Real Man*: "The answer to lust is love. Lust is degenerative, love is regenerative."[14] Lustful men, according to the Bible, are heartless, faithless, and merciless in their pursuit of personal pleasure at the expense of what is good or righteous (Rom. 1:26–32).

Lust is insatiable; love is easily satisfied. A man who loves his wife finds her easily satisfying, while a man who lusts for his wife never finds satisfaction from her despite how hard she tries. No matter how she cares for him, submits her body to him, cleans the house, takes care of the children, pays the bills, works at a job, she will never quench his lustful thirst. Why? Because lust is self-centered, while love is other-centered. Lust appeals to our greed, while love appeals to grace. Greed can never be satisfied; it always wants more. Grace finds satisfaction in the restoration and happiness of others. Once that is achieved, even if it comes in stages, grace finds satisfaction. Blessed is the wife who is lavished with grace rather than lashed by lust.[15]

Vice and the VCR

The videocassette recorder, hardly known until the early 1980s, has made sexually oriented material much more easily available and has brought it into many homes for the first time. Sales of hard-core porn videos more than doubled from 1983 to 1986.[16] In a survey of pastors published in *Leadership*, 20 percent said they look at sexually oriented media (print, video, or movies) at least once a month. Thirty-eight percent said they find themselves fantasizing about sex with someone other than their spouse at least once a month.[17]

My wife and I were northbound on the Golden State Freeway one day, climbing up the famous "Grapevine" which traverses the Angeles National Forest, when we became locked in a traffic jam several miles long. Radio news bulletins reported that a recreational vehicle had caught fire and could possibly ignite dry grass nearby. Several fire trucks were called. As we approached the danger area, we spotted a fireman friend of ours who was stationed with a fire company on the outskirts of Los Angeles. As we passed by we called out to him. He saw us and waved until we were out of sight, clasping his hands and holding them over his head. No one on the highway that day could possibly have known our special bond with him and our joy in seeing his victorious gestures. You see, he had confided in us earlier that God had answered his prayer to be delivered from the subtle addiction of pornography in the fire station where he worked.

X-rated videocassettes and cable programs offer idle fire fighters irresistible allurements. Our friend was at first shocked by them, then curious, and finally lured by these diversions during long stretches of boredom. For a long while he would keep away from it successfully. "But what was scary," he said, "was that it was *constantly* a battle—spiritual warfare. The thing that saved me was that I never quit fighting, although I was fighting it the wrong way."

Pornography was like alcoholism for our young friend—an addiction that required constant vigilance lest a passing look plunge the overcomer down the slippery slope and into the slough of despond. He found release at a retreat one summer where a friend made a covenant to pray with him concerning his struggle. Since then he has been careful never to return to pornography, although an occasional movie with nudity or a sex scene can be for him a source of temptation. He writes the following admonition to other men who might be enduring the same temptations:

> Acknowledge the sin and repent of it, claiming 1 John 1:9,10. If the sin seems to be oppressive in a demonic way, ask the Lord to break the bondage, and take a stand for truth. Do not give the devil an opportunity. Stay clear of that sin. Win the battle before the temptation begins by staying away from those things that tempt and keep spiritually fit. Read the Bible daily—verses like Romans 6:13 and 13:14, pray, be involved in church with brothers to whom you can be accountable.

Time to Come Clean

My good friend Keith Miller helped usher in a new era of truth-telling with his first book, *The Taste of New Wine*. I had the privilege of editing that book for Word Books and have since enjoyed reading all of Keith's books.

One of those books, *Habitation of Dragons*, includes the story of a deacon's conference sponsored by a large church where Keith was invited to speak. Keith brought with him two "witnesses" who talked frankly about the temptations of extramarital sex. But soon the pastor became nervous about continuing the subject. "Our men are dedicated Christians," the pastor said. "I know them personally. You'll offend them."

Keith retired to his room to rethink the program format, wondering how he might better minister to the dedicated deacons. Suddenly a knock came on the door. It was one of the deacons—he wanted to confess and pray. That night, four more "dedicated" deacons came to Keith to confess their sins and pray for forgiveness.[18]

I am grateful to God that I have not succumbed to sexual failures, although the temptations have been many. I recall, for example, being in a hotel room somewhere in the Midwest where two attractive women had a room next to mine. Twice as I passed their open door they invited me in. No one knew me there, and it would have been easy for me to fall prey to their enticements, but the Lord helped me to keep moving on.

Once as I was riding the elevator to a meeting in the Hilton Hotel here in Pasadena, a woman—perhaps in her early forties—wanted to know what floor I was going to. She suggested that I stop by her room and "visit" before going to my meeting. Again, God ordered my steps away from sin.

Another time, just after I arrived in a Calcutta hotel, a knock came on the door. A woman said she had been sent up from the desk to see if she could be of any help to me. Thank God, I was able to decline and close the door to my uninvited guest.

Let's stand against the tide, men—let's be different! Don't buy into the promotion of sex as mere physical enjoyment totally apart from the commitment of love. Men who open their Christmas present before the holiday invariably find themselves bored by the celebration.

For this is the will of God, your sanctification: that you abstain from unchastity; that each one of you know how to take a wife for himself in holiness and honor, not in the passion of lust like heathen who do not know God.

—*1 Thessalonians 4:3–5 (RSV)*

C TO CHASE RICHES

There's nothing in the world so demoralizing as money.
                              —*Sophocles*, Antigone

THREE

"Knowledge—Zzzzzp! Money—Zzzzzp! Power! That's the cycle democracy is built on!" wrote Tennessee Williams in the script of his 1945 play, *The Glass Menagerie*.[1] The lure of the "almighty dollar" is a major one. The love of money has destroyed homes, wrecked businesses, toppled careers, and shattered political ambitions. To get money, men will steal, horde, break up homes, lie, and sometimes kill.

Could you be tempted to compromise your honor in order to accumulate money? "He who hastens to be rich will not go unpunished," the Bible warns (Prov. 28:20). It has been my observation that some people who have money are poor, while others without it are truly rich. Some of the most insecure people I know have plenty of money. On the other hand, it is possible to be wealthier by doing without than by accumulating things.

The world says, "Get rich!" But our Lord says, Serve! *"He who is least among you all will be great"* (Luke 9:48, emphasis mine). Ralph Waldo Emerson made an important point when he wrote, "Give me health and a day and I will make the pomp of emperors ridiculous" (*Nature*, 1836). The Talmud carries this reminder: "When man enters life his hands are clenched but when he dies, his hands are open." To be sure, money isn't everything, but to some men the temptation to accumulate it is at the top of all coveted things.

Some of the people surveyed by the authors of *The Day America Told the Truth* confessed they would quickly lay aside their morality if the price was right. For the sum of $10 million:

- 25 percent would abandon their entire family;
- 25 percent would abandon their church;
- 23 percent would become prostitutes for a week or more;
- 16 percent would give up their American citizenship;
- 16 percent would leave their spouses;
- 10 percent would withhold testimony and free a murderer;
- 7 percent would kill a stranger;
- 6 percent would change their race;
- 4 percent would have a sex change;
- 3 percent would put their children up for adoption.[2]

Money or the Will of God?

I have a friend who was the president of a midwestern college when an experience made him realize how much the pursuit of money had crept into his career decisions. He was well into a ninety-day sabbatical given him by grateful associates when he was invited to become president of a university in California. Initially he and his wife rejected the offer. One reason was the lower salary at the new institution. Others included moving away from treasured friends and family, uprooting their children, and the many unknowns certain to surprise them.

Then one evening he and his wife rehearsed two themes upon which they had built their marriage and careers: 1) to praise God in everything they do, say, and experience, and 2) to hold loosely to everything, including careers, relationships, business interests, children, and educational pursuits.

"Why don't we make a list of reasons for and against making the move?" his wife suggested.

My friend went upstairs and typed out his list on his computer. A few minutes later he pulled the sheet from his printer and was stretched out on the bed reading it. Just then a call came from the head of the search committee at the university in California. The man on the phone listed the reasons why the school needed him. My friend was amazed to hear that the list the caller was reading largely matched his own list of reasons in favor of the move.

"We made the move," he said later, "never regretting for a moment taking the position with lower pay. So many good things have come to my wife and our children as a result that I hate to think we might have missed it for want of more money where we were."

The late Bob Jones, Sr., founder of the university in Greenville, South Carolina that bears his name, gave to each year's student body this ringing admonition: "Do right! Do right 'til the stars fall!" That exhortation, delivered with such intensity, has remained in the minds of many students through the years and, I'm sure, has delivered many from the worship of mammon.

Honesty's Rewards

Many years ago, an attorney friend of mine moved from the Midwest to California to continue his law practice. To be admitted to practice, however, he had to reside in that state for several months, pass the bar exam, wait several weeks for the results, and finally be sworn in. He was not supposed to practice law at all in California until he was admitted. As the months passed, however, living with a wife and children with no revenue became increasingly difficult for him. One day he received a call from a man who had been one of his clients in the Midwest. The man needed a contract drawn up quickly for a conference in Los Angeles. Because of his experience with the subject, my friend could have drafted it quite easily.

There would have been nothing morally wrong with doing the work. But the California State statutes and bar rules would have been violated had my friend carried out the assignment. The client was eager to make the deal and offered him generous compensation for the job. Yet, although my friend badly needed the revenue, he refused to accept the assignment. Reluctantly, the client got someone else to do the job. Several years later that same man was sent to a federal penitentiary for selling unregistered securities.

"My belief is that the illegal sale was negotiated and consummated in the meeting that I had declined to attend," the lawyer told me. "It is a foregone conclusion that the investigation and prosecution of the matter would have turned up my participation, with enormous adverse consequences to me."

Do right 'til the stars fall!
The temptation to go for the dollar instead of a client's best interests surfaced in New Mexico where a friend had accepted a position with a company that handled financial services. My friend wrote:

I enjoyed my position, but after working there for five months I began to realize that the policies my boss was proposing to his clients were very expensive when compared with other types of services that we sold. I ran all of the computer programs that generated the proposed insurance rates, as well as the commission income earned. It became quite clear that the commission held a much higher priority than what was economically better for the client. I prayed about the situation and asked the Lord for guidance.

My answer came on the day my boss requested that I lie to our insurance agency in Minnesota. A client had been denied medical coverage by other agencies because of his medical history. My assignment was to lie to our agency so that coverage would be accepted.

When I told my boss that I could not lie, I was soon laid off. However, the Lord cares for those who follow His Word and obey His voice. He had not forgotten me. I soon had new employment with more pay!

I faced the temptation to lie, stared it down, and learned a valuable lesson: God is always there to take care of us.

An American missionary in Italy was startled one day by the realization that he was a thief. He had seen himself as "a pretty correct Christian," but one day he knew something was wrong.

The problem surfaced while he was praying for guidance to correct some problems among other missionaries. Suddenly the Lord brought to his mind what he described as a "very sticky area in my life—stealing." How had it all happened?

In 1985 he and his wife had purchased a computer to help out with correspondence and ministry needs. From the outset the missionary resolved to do things the "tough" way by legally buying all programs. Things went well until he chanced upon a friend who had a similar computer system. This friend quickly and eagerly began offering help and advice with various problems and also gave the missionary copies of other programs.

The missionary rationalized, "I'm not the one copying the programs. I'm not distributing them, so why not use them? Isn't it really my friend's responsibility not to pirate? After all, I have told him before that I want to do things the right way." So the programs continued to arrive—sharp, helpful programs that became essential to the efficiency of the mission office in Italy.

Then the day of conviction arrived. "God broke through my self-justifications and showed me that my actions were none other than stealing and that I was a thief," the missionary said. "How could I go about correcting the problems of others when I was harboring dishonesty within myself?"

It would be hard to erase the programs and even more difficult to write the letter to his friend. But he made it clear nonetheless that any programs received in the future "would be looked at" to see if they could be useful, then would quickly be erased. He would keep only those which he could legally purchase.

Does he steal anymore? "I have noticed that I need to continually remind myself to erase those unpurchased programs," he says. "Sometimes the 'looking at' prolongs itself into days, weeks, and then months. Then the Lord convicts me that it's time to put the disk through the erase."

There is nothing wrong with wanting to save money and be efficient and prosperous in whatever work you are called to do. Indeed, prosperity is a divine idea—but the devil tries to destroy the joy of achieving it.

Throughout the Bible, prosperity looms as a divine promise: "Let the LORD be magnified, Who has pleasure in the prosperity of His servant" (Ps. 35:27). "Both riches and honor come from You" (1 Chron. 29:12). "And his [Joseph's] master [Potiphar] saw that the LORD was with him and that the LORD made all he did to prosper" (Gen. 39:3). In the parable of the talents, Jesus praised the servants who invested and multiplied their original investments, and condemned only the servant who hid his talent and made no effort to increase it. You see, Jesus never condemned riches—He condemned the rich for failing to obey God's laws.

The writer of Deuteronomy commands: "You shall remember the LORD your God, for it is He who gives you power to get wealth" (8:18). God is concerned about your bank account and material assets. He says through the prophet Isaiah, "I am the LORD your God,/Who teaches you to profit" (Isa. 48:17).

How much money would it take to satisfy a man? "Just a little more," say the wealthiest men on earth. The Bible answers them: "Those who desire to be rich fall into temptation and a snare, and into many foolish and harmful lusts which drown men in destruction and perdition" (1 Tim. 6:9).

The temptation to covet money is as old as humanity. It is not limited to people in slavery, victims of poverty, the ill and infirm, or people in debt. One of the most dramatic stories of a man who coveted riches is described in Joshua 7. It took place among the Israelites on the eve of the most exciting time in their history, just as they were entering into the Promised Land.

Following the miraculous defeat of Jericho, the Lord spelled out a clear warning to the Israelites not to take any of the spoils of Canaan. But Achan, the son of Carmi, could not resist them. During one of the battles he spotted a beautiful Babylonian garment, two hundred shekels of silver, and a wedge of gold weighing fifty shekels. He coveted them and hid them in his tent (Josh. 7:21).

Joshua knew something was wrong when the little city of Ai routed three thousand Israeli troops and killed thirty-six of them. Through a careful process directed by God, Achan was identified as the man responsible. He could not deny that he coveted what he could not have, took what he could not keep, and hid what he surely knew would one day surface and ruin him. He and his family and all of their possessions perished under a hail of stones, and Israel went onward, sanctified and ready for the challenges that lay ahead.

Every son holds in his hands his father's grey hairs and his mother's anxious heart; no power of nature can change that. An erring son is like the mother eagle that steals from the altar a piece of sacred flesh on which a smoldering coal clings. She brings it home only to burn up the nest and all her young ones in it.

The Subtle Temptation of Credit

Time after time I've seen men fall for the temptation to abuse credit available to them. Ironically, it is responsible, kind, good, and generous people who are given credit in the first place. And it is these who can think of the best ways to spend the money available to them.

Bill discovered this wonderful world of finance in the first year of his marriage. A college graduate, Bill enjoyed responsible employment in a solid company and was offered charge cards from several banks. *I didn't even ask for them!* he thought. *Isn't it wonderful?*

Soon, with the plastic cards in his pocket, he and his wife, Sherrilyn, were able to furnish their apartment much more quickly than they expected to. They filled their closets with more clothes and added some athletic equipment to their playroom.

When the first bills arrived, however, the couple was a bit concerned. The amounts were higher than they had expected. But at the bottom of each invoice was a line in small print which read, "Minimum Payment Due." Their concern quickly turned to satisfaction—they could pay that amount and still have money left over for their personal use!

Time passed, and the weary cycle of charges, with the ever-present interest on the money, became burdensome. They paid regularly, keeping their credit in good shape, but the payments on their cards soon took larger and larger chunks of their paychecks. The "minimum payments" did little to reduce the debt; it only paid the interest on the principal. You can guess what eventually happened: Bill and Sherrilyn had to consolidate their loans into a single, large loan in order to have smaller payments and eliminate their financial strain. But then their car needed repairs, so they used a credit card and the cycle began all over again.

I know a couple celebrating their fortieth wedding anniversary who are in the same precarious financial situation as Bill and Sherrilyn. Their only source of income now is their Social Security check. The husband had earned higher-than-average wages while his family was growing up. They had enjoyed a high standard of living and seemed to have everything—everything, that is, except a savings account. When the drought of retirement years arrived, my friend had no well to draw from.

When There Is No Proof

A tennis enthusiast I know—we'll call him Bruce—enrolled two of his children in weekly tennis lessons as part of their home schooling. After a few lessons, each time Bruce asked for a bill the instructor told him, "Oh, don't worry about it now. You can pay me later."

Months passed and the tab grew steadily larger. In April Bruce went to the club office again to settle up but the instructor, Tony, preferred to talk about tennis rather than the bill.

June came and again Bruce offered to pay his bill, congratulating himself on his honesty and goodwill in wanting to keep current. This time Tony asked, "When did you last pay your bill?"

Hadn't it been in April? Bruce thought. He couldn't say for certain, but Tony was ready to take his word for whatever Bruce's recollection was. Bruce told him he would look in his check register and be back on the following day. At home, however, Bruce could find no record of any payment by check. Neither could his accountant. Apparently nothing had been paid since December. Quick figuring by Bruce turned up a total of $1,000 still outstanding. The next time they talked, Tony suggested to Bruce that he look again in his check register to see for certain if he had paid the bill earlier.

I know why he wanted me to check my register, Bruce thought. *He wants me to find out what he already suspects—I owe him a thousand dollars! His good nature and my complacency have gotten me into this mess.*

Bruce easily could have lied to Tony and told him he had already paid his bill through April, even though he could not find a canceled check. But the more he thought about it, the more Bruce was convinced that he *hadn't* paid his bill in April. Temptation whispered, "Tony will take your word for it. You don't need to pay a thousand dollars." But Bruce's Christian commitment said, "You went in to pay your bill in April, but you have no record to show that it was paid—so you still owe the money."

One day Bruce was playing tennis with his pastor-counselor and realized he couldn't concentrate on the game. He was still tormented by the question: *Should I lie and save money, or tell the truth and pay the full amount?* Only when he decided he would pay the full amount was Bruce able to focus on his game. After that he enjoyed working up a good sweat while exchanging the ball across the net.

When Bruce went into the club office afterward, Tony seemed to be a little extra cordial, even uncustomarily loud in the good style of an enthusiastic coach. He uncharacteristically offered Bruce a soft drink while he hauled out his records. Bruce thought, *Uh-oh—he's being super friendly because in a few minutes he's going to be a lot richer and I'm going to be a lot poorer!*

Bruce watched as Tony opened his books, and to his amazement Tony said, "I just found that you paid *cash* in April, so I've deducted that amount from your bill. Your current bill is a little over three hundred dollars. Let's just round it out to three hundred."

"Tony was more honest than I," Bruce told me, "because he easily could have taken advantage of me. My heart leaped with joy. I had wrestled with this issue and settled on an honest response. Maybe the favorable outcome was because I had passed God's test by doing the right thing. Maybe it was because I had resolved always to be honest no matter what the cost. Most probably, it was both."

Pound Wise

More than fifty years ago, a man named George Clason wrote and published a series of pamphlets designed to teach readers how to handle money wisely. To illustrate his themes he used parables from the culture of ancient Babylon. These booklets have more recently been published as a single volume entitled, *The Richest Man in Babylon*. The rich man is named Arkad, and he is willing to share his secrets with all who are interested in learning the winning methods of his financial stewardship.

In the story, men throughout the East come to Arkad asking for his secrets of making money. His advice is remarkably simple:

"Some of you members, my students, have asked me this: 'How can a man keep one-tenth of all he earns in his purse when all the coins he earns are not enough for his necessary expenses?'" So did Arkad address his students upon the second day.

"Yesterday how many of thee carried lean purses?"

"All of us," answered the class.

"Yet, thou do not all earn the same. Some earn much more than others. Some have much larger families to support. Yet, all purses were equally lean. Now I will tell thee an unusual truth about men and sons of men. It is this: That what each of us calls our 'necessary expenses' will always grow to equal our incomes unless we protest to the contrary."³

The advice in this Babylonian proverb is as good today as it was when it was uttered in the ancient world of the Middle East. We always have good reasons to spend all we make. Lean purses or bank accounts prevent us from giving or saving, even prompting us to borrow beyond our capacity to repay. We need, as Arkad suggests, to "protest to the contrary."

The Samaritan's Perspective

The "Golden Rule" is our Lord's view of money. It modifies beautifully the life of the greedy: "Whatever you want men to do to you, do also to them, for this is the Law and the Prophets" (Matt. 7:12). The generous man is charitable, eager to forgive, humble toward all in every endeavor.

Such a man obeys the injunction: "Bless those who persecute you; bless and do not curse. Rejoice with those who rejoice, and weep with those who weep" (Rom. 12:14-15).

Terry Anderson and Tom Sutherlin, who were chained together many times during five years of captivity in Lebanon, could have become bitter enemies. Instead, they became lifelong friends according to a news release issued by *Writer's Digest*. They did this by obeying the admonition by the apostle Paul and being kind to their captors.

The more money we pay for an item, the more worth we attach to it. We get what we pay for and then value those items accordingly. For some, the person who has the most toys wins. But the fact remains that the man in the warehouse working for six dollars an hour is of no less value than the one in the suit and tie behind the glass upstairs. Inequities in pay do not make one person more or less worthy than another. On the other hand, pastors and preachers are "worthy of double honor" (1 Tim. 5:17), yet they are often very low on the pay scale.

Men invest money where their heart is—that is, where their concerns lie and in the causes they are most fond of. Edwin Louis Cole experienced lean years in the first few years of his ministry to men. Then he began to see how true the Lord's words were when He said, "For where your treasure is, there your heart will be also" (Luke 12:34). Instead of relying on offerings to support his ministry, Ed began charging a registration fee. Two things happened as a result: A strong financial underpinning helped to expand the ministry, and men began attending regardless of the weather. Obviously, men value and appreciate the things in which they have invested.

You can't build a church if its members don't invest financially in the ministry. Love never fails, but a sense of duty will.

Through obedience to Romans 12:15, a businessman can actually love a competitor who takes a bite out of his profits. A man can forgive an investor whose poor investment advice causes his financial resources to be lessened. A man can pray for another person who makes life difficult for him. Such a life requires hard work, sacrifice, and godly service.

"Give, and it will be given to you: good measure, pressed down, shaken together, and running over will be put into your bosom. For with the same measure that you use, it will be measured back to you" (Luke 6:38). This principle for people of the kingdom of God promises abundant returns in exchange for Christlike giving. In fact, it is *impossible* to outgive God. The apostle Paul roused his readers with these words: "He who sows bountifully will also reap bountifully" (2 Cor. 9:6).

Tithing, a minimum approach to giving for a dedicated believer, is thought by some to be a legalistic approach to giving. Indeed, God calls us to give spontaneously. "Well done, good and faithful servant; you were faithful over a few things, I will make you ruler over many things. Enter into the joy of your lord" (Matt. 25:21).

No man has any more time than any other. We can't *find* time for God; we must *take* time for God. God will not bless a man with prosperity simply so he can heap luxuries upon himself and his family. *He gives us prosperity so that we may use it to bless others who have needs.* Riches can curse as well as bless.

God Is No Man's Debtor

I serve as a board member of Focus on the Family, a ministry where financial matters are handled with the highest integrity. President James Dobson learned from his father the importance of handling money as a good steward. The senior Dobson often returned from his evangelistic crusades to report to his wife and son that he had given his honorarium to some family in great need. When the bills came, the elder Dobsons presented them to the Lord, reminding Him of the Scripture, "Give, and it will be given to you: good measure, pressed down, shaken together, and running over" (Luke 6:38).

As a child, Jim listened intently to those prayers and watched to see how the Lord would respond. He writes:

> I tell you without exaggeration that money invariably arrived in the next few days. God did not make us rich, as some ministers promise today. But He never let us go hungry. On one occasion, $1,200 arrived in the mail the day after family prayer. My childlike faith grew by leaps and bounds at this demonstration of trust and sacrifice by my father and

mother. I regret that my own children have never seen their parents forced to depend on God in the way I experienced as a boy.[4]

A graduate student in psychology at the University of Southern California told me: "Two things stand out when I recall the long talks I had with my dad during my troublesome teen years, because he said them so often. 'You can't out-give God,' and 'God is easy to live with.'"

Dr. Mark Lee, former president of Simpson College, said in a message at a Bible Conference that he believes a man's value system can be determined from the way he spends his money. It's also true, he says, that a man's value system can be determined from the way he *doesn't* spend his money, because stinginess is greed of the worst sort.

Hold loosely to material things, or whatever you own will eventually own you. One of the teenagers in Youth for Christ in the days when I was president of that ministry felt compelled to buy a car. His father offered to purchase a brand new four-door Chevrolet that was in mint condition. Imagining himself driving that big "family" car, the young man turned down the offer and scrimped and saved for an older, worn-out Mercury convertible that had many more miles on it. He thought he owned it—but the reality was that the car owned him, forcing his nose to the grindstone to pay for it.

Dennis Barnhart, president of the burgeoning Eagle Computer company, decided his company should go public with its stock. A neighbor of his in Palo Alto, California, a director of the Apple Corporation, told me that Dennis, age forty-four, became a multimillionaire virtually overnight, watching his ownership of 592,000 shares soar to $9 million. He bought a red Ferrari and stopped at a bar to celebrate that afternoon. At 4:30 P.M. he was heading home when he missed a curve, tore through a guard rail, and plunged to his death in a ravine.

When the Lord returns one day, how will He rate your life? How you spent your money could tell it all.

Spend your resources on things that will outlast your life. After all, you can take with you to heaven only your children and others whom you have told about Christ.

> *Why do you spend money for what is not*
> * bread,*
> *And your wages for what does not satisfy?*
> —*Isaiah 55:2*

S^{TO} EIZE POWER

You shall have joy, or you shall have power, said
God; you shall not have both.
—Ralph Waldo Emerson,
Journal, October 1842

I once asked a friend, "What would you do if you had all power and authority?"

He rubbed his hands together with pretended glee, smacked his lips, and began to list both sublime and ridiculous undertakings like a despotic neurotic.

We both laughed at his outlandish machinations. Then he told me, "I don't think I could handle all power and authority, but the One who had it could. He exercised it appropriately and toward appropriate ends. His life illustrates how power can be used and ought to be used. He never used His power selfishly. He never used it to strike back at those who maliciously misrepresented Him."

Jesus said to His disciples:

> You know that those who are considered rulers over the Gentiles lord it over them, and their great ones exercise authority over them. . . . Yet it shall not be so among you; but whoever desires to become great among you shall be your servant. And whoever of you desires to be first shall be slave of all. (Mark 10:42-44)

I was at home with my wife Dorothy when H. Ross Perot first hinted on a television call-in talk show that he would run for president if he received enough write-in votes to put him on the ballot. "Why," Dorothy asked, "would anyone want the job of President?" I gave my answer in five simple letters: "P-O-W-E-R."

Who's Got the Power?

Power is seeing ourselves as free from being coerced by others. If we feel our behavior is our own choice, then we feel powerful. But if we feel our behavior is determined by others, we feel weak.

Most men attempt to *feel* powerful to make up for their genuine *deficit* of power. Alexander the Great approached the pinnacle of power by wanting to conquer the world. Yet Jesus Christ, the most powerful man who ever lived, taught that the path to power was to want nothing: "Therefore do not worry about tomorrow, for tomorrow will worry about its own things" (Matt. 6:34). Alexander said, "*Lead* and be powerful." Jesus said, "*Serve* and be powerful."

If you desperately care what people think about you and equally desire for them to like you, then you have a lot less power than if you *didn't* have those worries. Conversely, if you don't care what people think, you'll have more power and less anger. The man with power is the one who doesn't care what happens tomorrow. In contrast, the man who worries about tomorrow feels weak because he is so dependent on other people for his power.

It's not so much how you behave that gives you power; it's how you see yourself. Show me a man who strives to be a millionaire, and I'll show you one who is almost totally controlled by others. He believes that when he becomes rich he will be powerful. But the truth is, only when he *gives up* the wish to be rich will he become powerful!

Power Plays

Men experience this strange thing known as power in virtually every human encounter. Salespeople make certain they put power at the center of every relationship. Books like Robert Ringer's *Look Out for Number One* and *Winning Through Intimidation* become best-sellers. Dale Carnegie puts power at the center of his classic book *How To Win Friends and Influence People.* Men who take his course on the same subject quickly learn that friendliness and courtesy give the appearance of a developing relationship. The prospective buyer then becomes vulnerable to the salesman's influence because of an innate desire to have a relationship with him.

The "battle of the sexes," so exploited by the media, seeks to determine who is stronger, male or female. And, indeed, many an argument between a husband and wife revolves around power. Most arguments over money are not about legal tender at all, but rather about who is going to control it. Arguments over children focus on whose influence will prevail. Arguments over clothes, household furnishings, vacations, what to watch on TV, when to mow the lawn, and where to live *all* have their seeds in who has power in the family.

Marital jokes that focus on the wife as "the boss" pinpoint this power struggle. Power is the central issue of male chauvinism as well as of radical feminism. Some men use the Bible as a weapon of intimidation toward their wives rather than as a guide for personal growth. In many cases, that practice is born out of fear. One of the worst agonies of powerlessness is experienced by the husband who tries in every way he can, but ultimately in vain, to prevent his wife from having an affair or falling in love with another man.

At social gatherings men thrive on conversations that reveal their grasp of trivia. Why? To have control over the conversation, to influence another person's emotions, to grab attention, to impress. No one knows how many acts of violence have erupted between men because each refused to admit to a power struggle.

Is there anything wrong with feeling weak? Not really. There are many situations over which we have no control at all. A man who is honest with himself will admit that at times he just wants to pull the covers over his head and weep. Our Lord knows that. He spoke directly to this need in Matthew 11:28: "Come to Me, all you who labor and are heavy laden, and I will give you rest." Jesus knows how little power we have over the events that touch our lives.

The death of a loved one, for example, can deal out a heavy dose of powerlessness in a man's life. So can disasters, burglaries, suffering, accidents, and skewed plans. Often we can't prevent any of these things, and each contributes to our sense of a lack of power.

To some, the thought of suicide offers an enormous sense of power. The idea that a person can actually choose how and when he is going to die allows him to seize power over his destiny. Some men can feel power in no other way. If they can't feel power in life, they reason, at least they can feel it in death.

Men in the public eye often strive mightily after power and adulation. They feel pressure to always attempt something bigger and better so they can outdo their last achievement. The Egyptian king Tutankhamen wanted to build the largest pyramid so he could have the best possible burial place— perhaps the height of megalomania! Sometimes it's hard to tell if a man is using his talents for the benefit of humanity or as a monument to his own narcissism. One way to find out is in observing how he behaves when he becomes frustrated in his attempts to build bigger and better things.

Such men don't really have power. On the contrary, their strong wishes for security and approval betray their weakness and insecurity. You see, many shows of power are simply a way to offset their weakness. Likewise, followers enjoy feelings of power by identifying with such a leader. This dangerous tendency is the cement that holds cults together, and it is present in many large churches as well.

Men define the word *power* in different ways. Warren Farrell gave it five components in his book *Why Men Are the Way They Are* :

1. Access to *external* rewards and resources (e.g., income, status, possessions) equivalent to the level of a person's expectation or desire.
2. Access to *internal* rewards and resources (e.g., inner peace, the capacity for emotional release, positive self-concept, alignment of overall values with daily activities, spirituality). Access starts with the awareness of the importance of these rewards, and becomes real with the time and ability to experience them on a level equal to one's expectation or desire.
3. Access to *interpersonal contact* (attention, affection, and love and respect from others, whether family or friends) equivalent to one's expectation or desire.
4. Access to *physical health, attractiveness,* and *intelligence* equivalent to one's expectation or desire.
5. Access to *sexual fulfillment* in a form that meets one's expectations.[1]

Power is often defined as "having control over one's life." Yet some "power brokers" might not be as powerful as they think. Does the stockbroker have control over his life when he is at the constant beck and call of his clients? Does the teenage ice skater have control over her life when she can't tell whether she is loved for herself or for her brilliant skating? Did my cousin in World War II have power over his destiny when a grenade exploded in his face? Does a physician have power over his life when he is a slave to his beeper?

"Power," write Fremont E. Kast and James E. Rosenzweig, "is the capability of doing or affecting something. It implies the ability to influence others. In its most general sense, power denotes (1) the ability . . . to produce a certain occurrence or (2) the influence exerted by a man or group, through whatever means over the conduct of others in intended ways."[2]

Everybody knows what physical power is. Most men would like more of that. Then there is material power. That's the kind a man thinks he has when he gives a large donation to an organization and then storms into the CEO's office to tell him how the company should be run. Finally, there is symbolic power—the kind I encourage leaders of organizations to use. It involves motivating associates to do their best to help an organization achieve its goals.

Lord Acton's comment to Bishop Mandell Creighton a century ago is heard often today: "Power tends to corrupt and absolute power corrupts absolutely."[3] Men who are in positions of leadership ought always to bear this in mind. They should welcome suggestions from boards of directors who insist on leadership accountability in handling money, people, and procedures.

Richard Foster addresses this point: "Those who are accountable to no one are especially susceptible to the corrupting influence of power. . . . Today, most media preachers and itinerant evangelists suffer . . . from the same lack of accountability that the wandering prophets of the sixth century did."[4]

Power and Authority

The concept of *power* is linked naturally to *authority*. Charles Colson writes,

> Power is the ability to affect one's ends or purposes in the world. Authority is having not only the power (might), but the right to affect one's purpose. Power is often maintained by naked force; authority springs from a moral foundation. Mother Teresa is the best living example. She spends her life helping the powerless die with dignity; yet few people command more authority worldwide.[5]

Worldly power—as defined by big bank accounts, buildings, or access to people in government—more often works against godliness; it does not foster it. *Power is authority.* "Authority," says John Gardner, "is legitimized power, i.e., a mandate to exercise power in a certain sphere. It is official or traditional sanction for individuals occupying specified positions to perform certain directive acts. . . . The meter maid has authority but not necessarily leadership."[6]

At some point you have probably encountered men who are driven to grab power and authority for selfish reasons. "Trust me," they say in businesses, colleges, and charitable organizations—and then we watch them nosedive into a quagmire of tragedy and loss.

A man with whom I once worked was invited to deliver the keynote speech at an important denominational meeting in his church. He later told me how hard it was afterward, when he returned to his family and friends, not to talk about the "importance" of his message. "The key to overcoming this kind of temptation," he said, "is to humble myself before the Lord, cultivate the attitude of a true servant like Jesus, and live under His lordship day by day."

Power in the Home

Many men brag about their wives and children, the money they earn, the committees they serve on, their skill in sports. But deep down many men feel totally inadequate for most tasks in their lives. Even though a man's admiring wife may stand genuinely proud at his side, he is constantly tempted to cover up his feelings with insensitive swagger or braggadocio.

Once when we were on a business trip, an associate confided to me that in his twenty years of marriage he never felt adequate to meet his wife's expectations of him in the home. I knew this man to be a good father and husband, a good provider, and a sensitive and caring Christian. Yet despite his achievements, he could not change his low concept of himself and accept his family's appreciation. Why not?

Men are tempted to place more satisfaction in achieving goals than in being a friend, a confidant, and a lover. Deep in our hearts, many of us feel inferior to women. Some men are intimidated by a woman's intuition about important decisions. She listens to her heart and makes sound decisions, while he painstakingly gathers all the evidence and then can't make up his mind about whether to choose column A or column B. I have stewed occasionally over decisions that from the beginning had been quite clear to Dorothy. She knew precisely what we ought to do all along.

Why is a husband tempted to react angrily when his wife greets him at the door with a list of things that need to be done around the house? The reason is that a man fears he is going to lose his freedom. His response baffles his wife; she has no clue as to how she could awaken any such fear in him. Nor does she have any desire to take control of her husband's life. On the contrary, most wives long for their husbands to feel free to exert their leadership as head of the home.

I like what C. S. Lewis wrote on the subject in his classic book *Mere Christianity:*

> Is there any serious feeling that the head should be the woman? . . . Even a woman who wants to be head of her own house does not usually admire the same state of things when she finds it going on next door. She is much more likely to say, "Poor Mr. X! Why he allows that appalling woman to boss him about the way she does is more than I can imagine." I do not think she is even very flattered if anyone mentions the fact of her own "headship." There must be something unnatural about the rule of wives over husbands, because the wives themselves are half ashamed of it and despise the husbands whom they rule.[7]

Does Father Always Know Best?

A mature Christian man is not tempted to think more highly of himself than he ought. He knows that he is not always right, and that the male is not the stronger of the sexes in every aspect of life.

Early in our marriage, my wife and I encountered a man who seemed to believe the exact opposite of this. He was determined to build up his own ego, much to the regret of all who lived near him. He had to be right in every conversation, and everyone whom he cornered had to listen to his mighty exploits.

Over time he began to slip increasingly into argumentative moods with his wife. He lost his temper often, finally becoming cold toward her and impotent in their sexual relationship. His children became openly unkind in showing they did not enjoy being with him.

Fortunately, this man woke up before his home was wrecked. He saw that his defensive behavior had contributed to his failed relationships. He started listening to his wife again. He began to risk being wrong in his judgments, and he allowed others to offer their opinions about decisions he had to make. Eventually he gave up his phony idea of manhood and accepted a more realistic view of himself. Sometimes being a strong man means having the ability to acknowledge failure, error, and weakness.

Unfortunately, father doesn't always know best, but he comes closest when he admits it.

Bowed Head or Clenched Fist?

When Jesus was handed the opportunity to show tremendous power at the start of His ministry, His response to the tempter was, "Away with you, Satan! For it is written, 'You shall worship the LORD your God, and Him only you shall serve'" (Matt. 4:10). Without hesitation, the Lord rejected the great temptation of power—it was His final blow against the enemy. And at that point the devil left Him and angels came to minister to Him.

It would be wonderful if we could face the enemy once, call on God to condemn him, and be free of him forever. But, unfortunately, life isn't that way. It wasn't in Christ's experience either. Satan left Jesus in the wilderness of temptation, but he waited and watched for another time to strike. Luke 4:13 says that after tempting Christ, the devil "departed from Him until an opportune time." He will do that with us as well.

An event occurred on January 21, 1930, which offers an illustration of what it means to be a wonderful instrument of power in this world, communicating the Word of the Lord to a needy generation. On that date, the most far-reaching radio broadcast up to that time was scheduled. It was the message of Great Britain's King George at the opening of the London Naval Arms Conference. The whole world was to hear the voice of the King for the first time.

Citizens of the United States almost missed it, however. Just before the King was to speak, a member of the control room staff of CBS radio tripped over a wire and broke it, severing connections. Harold Vivian, chief control operator, immediately grasped the ends of the broken wires, one in each hand, and restored the circuit. The volts of electricity shook his arms and went through his entire body, but he held on until new wires were connected. The King's message went out across the sea to an entire nation through the tingling body of Harold Vivian.[8]

The King of kings has a message for men in our sinful, hurting world: The circuit has been broken—sin has cut us off from God's voice and left us in silence. But, men, you and I are in a position to close that circuit with hearts made pure by prayer and obedience. Our lives are meant to bring our King's message to all who will hear!

Do you find yourself at the peak of your career today, with plenty of money and prestige? Do you love for people to wait on you? Do you enjoy having power and authority? Watch out! If you listen closely, you'll hear the hiss of the serpent; he is waiting nearby for his opportunity to make you fall. It won't be difficult for him. All he needs is for you to adopt the lifestyle he offers, and suddenly you will be facing the greatest fall you've ever had.

Will you face such temptation with a bowed head or a clenched fist? Will you say, "Nobody tells me what to do!" Or will you pray, "Not my will, Father, but Thine be done." Your worldview has room only for one.

> *Whoever wants to be great among you must be your servant. And whoever wants to be greatest of all must be the slave of all.*
>
> —*Mark 10:43-44(TLB)*

A TO BE NGRY

Give not reins to your inflamed passions;
Take time and a little delay;
impetuosity manages all things badly.
                    —Statius-Thebais[1]

FIVE

Anger is often a man's first emotion—and it is equally often his last. Anger is God-given; we cannot be fulfilled without it. Like love, anger is woven into the warp and woof of our being. Thomas Fuller called anger "one of the sinews of the soul."[2]

Misguided men are tempted to use anger to wound and destroy. Mature men use anger to halt injustice, promote growth, and establish values. Passive men who have no anger care little about love and cannot experience much joy.

Anger begins early. A baby could not turn over in its crib without anger. A musician could not write a great score of music without an anger at mediocre melodies. Dictators would continually run roughshod over the less powerful, except for the anger in good men that causes them to rise up and stop the evil. David could not have written the imprecatory psalms without sanctified anger.

On the other hand, suppressed anger interferes with warm human relationships, robbing a person of a happy, fulfilling life. This kind of anger comes from the frustration of facing things that are not as you want them to be, yet refusing to accept them as they are. Anger must be involved constructively in the process of changing, destroying, or accepting those things.

"Most men recognize their anger; many do not, or can't admit it," writes Dr. S. Philip Sutherland. "A man can be angry and not even know it; another can know it and be unable to express it; still others can be angry and neither know it nor express it."[3]

The fallout from anger can take many forms. Among these are the following emotions:

Feelings of Weakness

A bleary-eyed young man with an unwashed face and dirty clothing burst into the office of a church in Southern California and asked to see the pastor. The pastor showed the visitor into his office.

The young man took the chair offered him and sat rigidly on the edge of it, obviously agitated. His nervous hands moved back and forth from one knee to the other. "What would you do if I brought a gun in here and threatened to use it?" he asked. His eyes brightened at the prospect.

The pastor felt a chill creep up his spine. He recognized the syndrome—a man with no power, wanting to dominate the world. "You don't need a gun to be accepted here," the pastor began. "There is a better way to get rid of weakness and feelings of powerlessness."

"That's not true!" the young man shot back. "My way is a lot better and a lot more certain." This angry young man's emotions offered him only the terrible reality of weakness, which he wanted to avoid at all costs. For weak men such as he, anger offers strength for a season. That day in the pastor's study, the visitor was introduced to another source of strength, competence, and security. I don't know whether he continued to reinforce his false sense of power with a gun (or even if he had one), but I do know that at least he was given a glimpse of the remedy for the feelings destroying him.

Loss of Self-sufficiency

Not every man with explosive anger wants to dominate another person. Sometimes a man just wants to regain the feeling of self-sufficiency he lost growing up. Such a man often cannot resist fulfilling the imposed wishes of others and becomes easily dominated. But out of that impulse and repeated experience comes a rage that can drive him to regrettable acts.

A man was sawing boards to hang shelves in his garage when a neighbor offered to help. "Bug off!" the man snapped back. "I don't need your help."

The retort offended the neighbor, and he hurried away, reminding himself never to make the offer again. What he didn't know, however, was that the Saturday carpenter had been told all his life he would amount to nothing. "You're a dummy," his father told him repeatedly. "I don't know what you'll ever do in life to make a living."

Consequently, the son grew to adulthood without ever letting down his guard. To be sure, he was intelligent, and he understood that his angry responses were illogical. But at a level too deep to change easily, he feared his desires and his needs. So when he was threatened, he retreated into his fort, fired off his guns of anger, and felt self-sufficient again.

Loss of Importance

The young man in the pastor's study was angry because he was hungry for power. The Saturday carpenter was angry because he wanted to restore his self-sufficiency. Another type of man becomes angry to try to restore his rights. You'll see him gripping the steering wheel of his car, cursing other drivers for their stupidity. If you were to ask him, "Why do you become so angry out on the road?" he'd answer, "Because there are so many stupid drivers out there."

"Why do 'stupid drivers' make you angry?"

"Because they get in my way!"

Soon you'll discover that the man who is hungry for power on the highway wants to be the center of attention in everything he does. Perhaps he grew up in a home where doting parents gave him everything he wanted, and now he expects the world to treat him the same way. He chooses to be angry rather than to admit that, in truth, he has no more rights than the next person.

Loss of Perfection

Next is the man who is angry because he can't admit to himself or anyone else that he's not perfect.

For a man named Brad, this came to light on the tennis court, where he constantly threw his racket in a fit of rage. He had played tennis since he was seven, taken lessons from the finest certified professionals, and considered himself an expert. And he desperately wanted to keep that image of himself.

But tennis balls, even for top players, don't always go where they're supposed to. Brad desperately needed to play a perfect game—so when he failed to serve the ball over the net with precision, he blamed his opponent or the weather or the uneven court.

What will eventually become of this young man? Either he will learn to relax and surrender his fantasy, or he will drive harder for the illusion (or, perhaps, he will join a social activist crusade in order to lash out at society!). If he is like most perfectionists, Brad would rather remain "perfect" and blame other people for his mistakes.

Myths Concerning Anger

Most of us know anger when we see it. You've probably known men who are so angry they have to keep a smile on their faces, a tease on their tongues, or their chair empty in social circles where there is the danger they'll be revealed as less than perfect.

Following are five myths that men generally hold about anger:

Myth 1: Anger shows only in actions.

Angry men do not always strike out at people and things. More often they go along with the game plan, teasing, playing practical jokes, perhaps pinching a little too hard, and reluctantly forgiving others (but rarely forgetting what they did).

"He doesn't seem to be angry," his friends might say. Or, "I can't figure out why he did that—good ol' Bill. It just doesn't fit with him." Often the angry man himself is not aware of his rage.

Angry men respond to situations in different ways. Let's say a bank mistakenly overcharges interest on four customers' credit card accounts. One man storms into the bank and gives the manager a tongue-lashing. The second man phones the bank and mumbles his displeasure to whoever answers the phone. The third man stuffs the monthly statement into the files and forgets that it ever happened. And the fourth man justifies the mistake by explaining that the bank was being sold, and that the records "just got mixed up a little bit."

The first two responses represent angry behavior. The third and fourth responses are examples of angry *feelings*. The first two did something about the mistake; the latter two denied it and tried to justify the mistake. If you asked the latter two if they were angry, they probably would deny it—because they probably wouldn't even know it!

Myth 2: Men are always aware of their anger.

Denny, a truck driver, sat at the counter of his favorite cafe with his hands clenched. "You look mad," the waitress said as she brought his water, napkin, and coffee. Denny frowned at her, took a sip of coffee, and put the cup back down on the saucer a little too hard. "Me? I'm not angry," he said with a tight laugh. "Why should I be angry?" He turned to the manager of the cafe. "You hear that, Joe? Micki says I'm mad. What would I be mad about, huh? I'm *not* mad, Micki."

A man in a booth at the same restaurant left a meager tip. Outside he began blasting his air horn repeatedly, because a car was parked in front of his rig so that he couldn't move.

A third man in the restaurant said nothing when some catsup from the waitress's tray smeared his freshly cleaned suit. Later he told his wife, "I was so mad, I could have killed her!"

The first man was angry but did not know it. The second man was angry and expressed it. The third had felt his anger but did not express it.

Myth 3: Righteous indignation is not anger.

There is nothing wrong with being righteously indignant. Sometimes anger is indeed justified. Even our Lord was angry when He cleansed the temple of the money changers. But justification for anger doesn't change the fact that indignation *is* anger. Throughout the Bible, God expresses anger when people don't put Him first or they give Him second place to matters they consider more important.

Many times people who think they are righteously indignant blame others for their anger. They are "too stupid," "too morally depraved," or "too unwilling" to face the consequences of their actions. Just as often, however, these complainers are angry not righteously, but merely because others didn't treat them as they thought they should be treated.

Elijah, in 1 Kings 18, grew angry because the people of Baal didn't answer him when he demanded that they choose between the true God and their idols. Elijah handled his anger in a mature manner. He didn't do any of these things with a quivering chin or a pout, but with the kind of anger that rises from good judgment, concern, and patience. He used force that was available to him, and God was glorified.

Myth 4: *Anger can be accumulated and stored up.*

For many years, psychologists thought anger could be stored up in a person's heart through repeated encounters until its head of steam was so great it would "blow." That view is no longer held by many of our psychologist friends. They say that what is really at work in the mind of a man who is headed for an explosion is the feeling of lessening power, lessening importance and/or perfection, and lessening control. To retrieve these feelings, most men lash out in desperation with the one tool they know will work: anger.

A man is already late for work when a car pulls out in front of him on the boulevard and makes him slow down. Then he misses the green light at the intersection ahead, and he becomes more angry. As he pulls into the alley to park his car, a large truck sits blocking the thoroughfare. Finally, when he steps into his office, he "explodes" in anger at his secretary in order to get back some of his power, self-sufficiency, and "perfection."

Myth 5: *Angry men aren't responsible for their behavior.*

"I was so mad, I couldn't see straight!" angry men have said. Or, "It wasn't *my* fault. I just lost my temper." Or, "Don't blame your father. He's just mad."

There is abundant evidence to show that angry men do indeed know what they are doing. One enraged husband smashed everything on the fireplace mantel *except his favorite mug*. Another man grabbed his gun during a family quarrel and took careful aim at the heart of each member as he clicked the trigger. The gun didn't go off because the day before he had carefully removed the bullets. He had seen his fury coming and didn't want to kill his family; he just wanted "to teach them a lesson."

The nation's courts today wrestle with whether people who lose control of their mind through rage are responsible for their behavior. Without question, anger is a choice—but most angry men deny their anger. They call it "frustration," "teasing," or "just a desire to set wrong things right."

The Biblical Way to Handle Anger

One of the humblest men I know is my beloved friend Bill Bright, founder and president of Campus Crusade for Christ International. Bill has a devoted wife, children who love him, and a unified staff in all parts of the world, and all are happy to have a part in his God-given vision for evangelism and discipleship.

When I asked Bill whether he ever faced temptation, he quickly responded with this letter:

Some time ago, I was faced with a crucial decision that involved the announcement of a special project we were launching. It came to my attention a little before 5 P.M. that we needed desperately to do a special mailing. To this end I picked up the telephone and asked one of my associates to inquire if a particular department could help us that evening to mail out the urgent information. My associate called back to say that they were not available. It was almost five o'clock and everybody was going home, and therefore there was no one around to help me on this project.

I became a bit impatient and decided to call the head of the department myself to express my concerns that they were not available. Unfortunately, I came across a bit dictatorial, explaining to him that the ministry of Campus Crusade for Christ was a calling, not an eight-hour-a-day job, and that in light of the urgent project that needed to be undertaken, I expected them to be as available as I to complete it. Obviously, that was not the right approach. In the process, I offended my brothers who were involved in the project, and soon my verbal insensitivity was passed all around the department and beyond.

The Lord convinced me that I should go to them and ask them to forgive me for my impatience. I went to meet with the people involved. I apologized to them and shared my regrets and we had a love feast. God turned what could have been tragedy to triumph and discord to harmony and blessing. The greatest power in the world is love and "Love is very patient and kind, never jealous or envious, never boastful or proud, never haughty or selfish or rude. Love does not demand its own way. It is not irritable or touchy. It does not hold grudges and will hardly even notice when others do it wrong" (1 Cor. 13:4–5 TLB).

All men struggle with feelings of inferiority in some area of their life. But sometimes their cover-up is worse than their weakness. Men can look ridiculous in their futile attempts to hide inadequacies—whether it's in trying to meet the needs of family, keep up with tasks despite energy drain, confront an individual who's hard to talk to, break a habit or an addiction, face surgery that could mean the discovery of a fatal illness, struggle in a difficult marriage, care for aging parents, complete academic pursuits, or live with a disability. What man wants to be insufficient, incapable, unable?

Sanctified Anger

In looking for satisfaction and rewards, men often turn to their work rather than to people—including their own families. It is in this area that men must take decisive action to find balance and fulfillment. This holds true *especially* for men who are in full- or part-time service to the Lord.

An associate pastor at a large church in California speaks of an experience that provided him with a lesson he passes along at every opportunity. It wasn't until he became angry at his own excesses that he finally determined to exchange them for a more fulfilling and fruitful life.

Early in his ministry he became so absorbed in his work that he had no time for renewing his spirit. He worshiped, he says, "the goddess of success." Without seeing where his frenetic pace was taking him he filled his schedule with early-morning "power breakfasts," two-hour lunches, and frequent phone calls to his wife and children to report that he would be skipping supper because he didn't have time to eat before yet another meeting. But he was *successful!* he emphasizes.

"Busyness was my goddess," he says, "a full calendar was my Bible, and a prayerless rushing was my way of doing God's will. After four very 'successful' years of living like this, the sin of activity overwhelmed me. My most precious and important time of the day—time in the early morning with the Lord—was gone. My beautiful wife and three wonderful kids had developed their own priorities without me, and told me so. I suddenly became aware that I was *doing* for God, but I wasn't *being* with Him. Maybe, just maybe, God was not pleased by my priorities." Still, he thought all the time, *who could argue with success?*

That pastor might still be alone in the fast lane today if not for a simple question asked by a parishioner one day: "When was the last time you got alone with God and experienced His presence?"

My friend was stunned. He mumbled something like, "I'm too busy getting things done for God to take that kind of time."

To him, sitting quietly in a secluded place and experiencing the Lord's presence seemed selfish, a waste of time. How could he get through his commitments at the church office by sitting somewhere alone, contemplating God?

Before long, however, he was doing just that. He began setting aside one afternoon a week to visit a special place in the mountains where he could commune with the Lord of the universe. He continued that practice for an entire year.

"I now worship the Lord of priorities, the God of peace, first," he says, "and I look at my calendar afterward."

By abandoning his cover-up, that pastor has gained a renewed desire for ministry—and is seeing fruit in his labors that he never knew was possible. He has peace. His wife and children have a husband and father who has both energy and time. "Now," he says, "I never want to return to worshiping the idol of busyness again."

Anger Under the Clerical Collar

An older theological student who graduated from seminary not long ago was led by God to organize a church renewal ministry. His group began to flourish, and soon he was receiving more calls than he could handle.

Before becoming a follower of Jesus Christ, this man had carried a gun as an officer of the federal government and was trained to "neutralize" any injustice. With firepower and the authority to use it, he wasn't accustomed to putting up with any insolence when he was behind a badge.

Unfortunately, his lightning temper carried over with him from his old life as a non-Christian to his new life in ministry. At one point he served as an interim pastor at a church in San Diego. This required a commute, and one Saturday on his way to the church he stopped at a Jack-in-the-Box restaurant. He ordered a burger and sat down with it and a book.

Two teenage boys entered the near-empty restaurant and sat down at the table next to him. Before long, the boys became loud and vulgar. The pastor turned and asked them nicely if they could "keep it down to a dull roar" since he was trying to read. One of the boys answered, "If it's too loud for you, go outside, you old bag."

My friend shot out of that booth like a rocket. He grabbed the boy by his belt and collar and slammed him against the wall. Taco shells and soft drinks went flying as the young man fell to the floor. Chairs were overturned, tumblers broken. When it was over, the pastor realized he had just committed assault against two minors. "Me—a pastor!" he said later incredulously, hardly able to believe his own story.

He quickly calmed himself and helped the young man up. The boy was as frightened as the pastor was embarrassed. "Finish your lunch, what's left of it," the preacher said and returned to his table.

Sitting down, he was deeply convicted about what he had just done. When he looked at his book, ironically entitled *When a Man's a Man*, he was convicted further. He had not been a man—he had been a bully. He got up, went over to the two boys and asked their forgiveness, explaining that he should not have exploded. Then he left and drove to San Diego where he was scheduled to preach the following day.

As he drove along, the pastor decided he would have to confess to his board members what he had done and ask them to advise and discipline him.

That evening, a special board meeting was called, and the pastor explained what had happened. Some on the board were involved with military forces based in San Diego, and several supported his actions. Because of this, a time of teaching was required until all agreed that the pastor's action was sinful.

The board decided that night that since the pastor had confessed, he should be allowed to preach on the following day. The worship service that morning was charged with emotion. Afterward, a number of people who also had fallen to the temptation of anger responded to the call to confess and make things right.

"Confessing our sins one to another and bearing one another's burdens really does fulfill the law of Christ," said the pastor, referring to James 5:16 and Galatians 6:2.

A decade later, after serving in various ministerial capacities, that pastor was asked to provide expertise to help set things right in a church where the congregation had suffered from poor leadership. When one of the deacons commented that this man was "perfect for the job," the ex-police officer felt moved to share his embarrassment about the time his temper clouded his judgment and nearly brought the law down on him.

"I am not perfect," he began. "I may not embarrass this church with drunkenness or womanizing or embezzlement. But my compulsive behavior toward insolence could land me in jail and bring reproach on the church. Let me confess to when I became a 'jack in the box.'"

Every member listened carefully, and each was asked to respond. All the men—some with tears—thanked the pastor for his honesty. "We are even more convinced that you're perfect for this interim position," they said. "We need someone who will be transparent, not 'holier than thou.'"

Lying As a Form of Anger

The president of a Christian college once carefully interviewed a man who was being invited to teach the Bible on its radio outreach. "Is there anything in your life that might embarrass the Lord, His Church, or this school?" the president asked pointedly.

"There is nothing," the candidate replied. "I have kept myself pure for the Christian ministry."

But within a year his past caught up with him. For half a decade this married minister had been having an affair. He left the broadcast, and his pulpit, in disgrace.

The results of surveys by James Patterson and Peter Kim in their book *The Day America Told the Truth* show that 91 percent of Americans lie regularly. Most Americans find it difficult to get through a single week without lying. One in five can't make it through twenty-four hours without conscious, premeditated lies.[4]

Men tell women they love them to get what they want. Men lie to their parents about being homosexual. Men are not honest with their wives about their affairs or even about having children out of wedlock.

Men also lie when they violate their beliefs. Children are quick to pick up on this, as the following story illustrates:

A distraught father complained to his pastor that his son was continually disobedient. His son would not heed his admonitions to stop telling lies, getting the boy into a lot of trouble.

The father invited the pastor to lunch to talk things over. As the father was driving with the pastor to a restaurant, he ran a red light, chuckled, and said, "I got the city on that one." He ran another red light and again treated the offense with nonchalance.

At that point, the pastor asked the man to stop and let him out of the car. He did stop—puzzled—and the pastor got out of the car. He made his point clear that at least *he* was going to submit himself to the authority of civil government, which is commanded in the Scriptures.

"Don't expect your son to do anything but follow your example of dishonesty and cheating," the pastor warned.[5]

Anger in Cover-ups

I once worked with a man who hedged the truth about his athletic prowess. When asked if he had participated in sports in college, he would say he ran track under the tutelage of the famous coach Gil Dodds, who broke records in indoor track in 1947. Yet the truth was that although this man had trained all summer to get in shape for college track in September, he attended only three days of the school's track and football camp—and he did so poorly that he elected not to continue even under Gil Dodd's training.

One of my high school classmates back in Cleveland, Ohio, tried out for the basketball team. It was very important to him to make the team, because being an athlete meant instant popularity with girls. Unfortunately, the coach cut him during tryouts. The experience was so traumatic that the young man quit sports altogether and never tried out again. But he still held sports in high esteem, so whenever someone asked about his involvement with athletics he felt like a failure unless he lied about his record. Eventually, he realized athletic ability does not determine a man's worth—that is wrapped up in our relationship with God alone. The man dropped his facade and began telling the truth—and today he can laugh at his lack of skills in sports!

Where Anger Starts

Ideally, a boy learns how to be a man from the example of his father and the loving counsel of his mother. David Stoop and Stephen Arterburn point out in their book, *The Angry Man*, that boys often, however, receive the wrong signals from their fathers. Many men are so busy earning a living and making sure their wives and children have a comfortable life-style that they fail to provide nurturing relationships with them, with friends, and with God. Their sons may become angry as they grow to adulthood, because the message they have received is that they must work long hours, make a lot of money, and seek promotions in order to be an adequate father. A mother can perpetuate the myth by subtly excusing the father's negligence, telling her son what a wonderful daddy he has: "He works hard so we can have nice things."[6]

The role models in TV and film do little to point a young man in the way he should go. The larger-than-life individuals have a lover in every port and never suffer from guilt, paternity suits, or venereal disease. If a hero of this sort doesn't get his way, he flattens his opponent without remorse. And if his boss doesn't measure up, he punches him and walks off the job. For a young man who's desperate for an example to emulate, trying to live up to such wild misrepresentations surely leads only to frustration and anger.

What is the answer? Men need first to be honest with their families and to acknowledge their weaknesses. This paves the way for them to receive from their families the affirmation they need as they struggle to provide for them. In turn, men need to provide the love and care their wives and children need in everyday family activity. A man's lack of self-control, his social immaturity, unrealistic expectations, feelings of low self-worth, guilt, fear, and confusion in his roles strain relationships for everyone. And this behavior can only send the wrong message to our sons about what a man should be.

Ron R. Lee attributes enormous frustration among men today to the role revolution in America. He writes:

> In generations past, spouses found security in established roles. Men toiled for the daily bread; women baked it and served it to the family. But during the past quarter-century, all the rules have changed. More women have entered the work force, and they are taking advantage of new opportunities in the fields of business, finance, politics, even the military. For every Alan Alda who salutes today's "new women," there are a host of ordinary Joes who are bewildered, and sometimes threatened, by women who demand to be treated as equals in the workplace as well as at home.[7]

What's an Angry Man to Do?

A man may begin to sense that he represses anger, has a destructive temper, or suffers pain and fatigue from unresolved frustrations. As he becomes aware of these things, he can take the following steps toward healing:

Pray

Prayer brings changes. Praying about a problem is, first of all, an admission that there is a problem. It also is an admission that the problem is within, not without. Praying moves away from blaming others and leads to humility. This opens up to us the divine guidance of the Holy Spirit.

Be honest

A child lives in a world of unreality. Food appears daily; clothing is hung in his closet; protection is always at hand. All of these wonderful things are taken for granted. In a child's mind, they happen merely because he wants them to happen.

When the time comes for kindergarten, the child's fairy-tale view of the world is shattered. Suddenly another child kicks him simply because he wants to play with a toy he has. His parents never did that!

Each time reality offers hard truth, a person experiences anger and sadness. Thus, for a man to refuse to believe the truth is to invite anger. By mourning, on the other hand, we acknowledge our losses and through the years move toward a realistic view of the world. Eventually we can enjoy life as we have it rather than protesting vainly against what we don't have.

Confront

Without judging, state clearly where you stand. Speak the truth *in love*—that is, with gentleness toward others and with their welfare in mind. Admit anger, guilt, wrong desires, and shortcomings. Ask others to give you their impressions of you. Do not become angry or try to defend yourself; do not try to justify your wrongdoings or failures. Most of all, do not try to talk another person out of his impression of you. Remind yourself that he or she is merely giving his or her own biased impression of you. Only you can sort out the truth from their motives, needs, and fears—and from your own. So if half a dozen friends say you appear to be angry, believe them!

Accept

For the rest of your life you will be called upon to accept yourself as you are—that is, as God made you—even though you may feel unacceptable. Give up all childhood fantasies of nobility, popularity, strength, wealth, and skill. Face life as it is.

Cultivate a friend who will accept you even though you aren't as great as you pretended to be. Men don't reject a friend who approaches them in this way; they only reject the man who attacks in some way or continues to hold up facades. Acknowledge your unrespectable and unlovable parts, and you will be loved and appreciated.

Anger will be your companion for life. Use it to motivate yourself and to accept reality. Use it for growth and strength. Don't allow it to alienate and destroy.

> *"Call for the grandest of all earthly spectacles, what is that? It is the sun going to his rest. Call for the grandest of all human sentiments, what is that? It is that man should forget his anger before he lies down to sleep."*[8]

P TO BE ASSIVE

Those who say "I will" accomplish everything;
those who say "I can't" fail in everything.

SIX

In the face of exciting opportunity, many men are tempted to take the easy road and not accept a challenge. This perplexing thing known as passivity, sometimes seen as "shyness," is a problem for many men—but it can be an even worse problem for their frustrated wives and business associates. Dr. Philip G. Zimbardo, a faculty member at Stanford University, calls it a "social disease."[1] Trends seem to indicate that passivity and shyness among men are going to become worse in the coming years as social forces increase their isolation, competition, and loneliness.

But the fact remains that, behind our boasting, our can-do image, and our athletic daring, a lot of us men are shy. We encourage our wives to fulfill our social responsibilities while we sneak out the back door to shoot some baskets, crawl under the car to change the oil, or sink into our favorite chair in the den to watch a game.

Nathaniel Hawthorne may have had the shy man in mind when he wrote: "What other dungeon is so dark as one's heart? What jailer so inexorable as one's self?"[2]

My friend Roosevelt Grier, the former Los Angeles Ram and a mountain of a man who would seem to fear nobody, almost became mute in school when other kids laughed at his size. One of my associates at World Vision was so shy as a youth that he actually dropped out of high school early in the ninth grade. He later obtained his diploma through high school equivalency tests and today has degrees from both college and seminary.

Shy people usually fit into one of the following five basic classifications: shy-dependent, shy-aggressive, shy-terrified, shy-anxious, and shy-contented. Many of these categories overlap one another; probably no person fits into only one. Men, if you spot yourself passing in review in any of these five divisions, report for duty at the changing of the guard and let the High Command know that one soldier wants to join the ranks of the transformed and prepared!

Shy-Dependent

Most timid men belong to this category. *Shy-dependent people* generally are helpful, cooperative, and kind. They rarely show anger. When people describe such a man they usually say, "He's nice, but I don't know much about him."

Men who are shy-dependent see themselves as weak and others as strong and capable. Their passivity and apparent helplessness are unconscious techniques to force others to take care of them, protect them, advise them, and comfort them. These types of men never move far from their comfortable, passive role. To act assertively by expressing an opinion or by sharing a feeling or by being responsible would mean losing their position as helpless children; other people might no longer act as their strong protectors or supporters. They are assertive only in their fantasies. Outwardly they remain passive so they can continue clinging to the hope that their fantasies might someday be fulfilled.

Shane was a classic shy-dependent. Raised by his mother, a grandmother, and an aunt (each competing to see who could be the best "mother" to him), he developed extreme passive tendencies. Shane wanted the whole world to treat him as his maternal trio had.

Eventually Shane was married, but he remained passive. His wife disciplined the children, ran the home, and budgeted and spent the money. His corporation told him what time to show up for work, what jobs to do, and what roles to fulfill.

His wife was patient until their three daughters became teenagers. Then her patience dissolved. She even threatened divorce—but Shane still remained the quiet listener, the nonaggressive lover, the silent wallflower at parties, moving through life behind a mask that read: "This is just the way I am."

Although a Christian, Shane was passive about the passages of Scripture that admonished him to provide leadership for his family. Occasionally he did try to lead, but because his efforts were so painful, Shane felt he was only artificially trying to conform to biblical standards. Friends and observers saw him mostly as almost a nonentity within the family.

Finally Shane's wife threatened to leave him unless he gave her more support and acted more assertively with her and the children. In spite of this threat, Shane remained passive; he kept to his usual attitude of, "It will all work out." He could not see how his shyness caused his wife such frustration. He simply was behaving in the way he had behaved toward women all his life, and he'd never seemed to have these problems with them. He didn't understand, however, that he was asking his wife to act like his mother. And she wanted a husband, not a son!

Whenever Shane was forced into being assertive, he became angry and depressed because he feared losing his security as a passive-dependent child. To avoid these moments Shane remained a nice, quiet, reliable individual, neither friendly nor unfriendly, and somewhat invisible in social situations. He did his work well. Overall he experienced little anxiety because he was able to maintain his passive position both at home and at work.

A lot of men are like Shane—*uninvolved*. They appear placid and agreeable, but they behave this way only to be allowed to *remain* uninvolved. Whenever they are asked or expected to lead, a torrent of anxiety, fear, and anger is released. They immediately do things that are designed to get them out of the active position. They change the subject, feign tears, complain of illness, leave the room, or get others to talk or make jokes.

Shy-Aggressive

This label may seem to present a contradiction. In clinical psychology this category is commonly identified as *the passive-aggressive personality*. Such men manipulate others with a shy-passivity that stems from a fear of being manipulated and ultimately a fear of being unloved. They have a strong need to ward off the aggression of others, and their passivity helps them do just that. They know their shyness in certain situations is an irritant to other people, and they often come away from such situations with a sense of smug victory. It's as if they say, "Aha! I won because you weren't able to dominate me." Life becomes me-versus-them.

Listen to this candid comment from one shy-aggressive man: "When people come at me strongly, I just sit there and don't pay attention to what they're saying. With a very passive expression on my face, I let them rant and rave, and I feel very, very smug."

Shy-aggressive men do not allow themselves to feel needy or loving toward others. They equate feeling needy with feeling weak. Shy-aggressive persons believe that if they allow themselves to love, their beloved will have power over them. When others have something shy-aggressive men want (such as love), those others are seen as powerful. So rather than allow themselves to feel love toward them, shy-aggressives deny those feelings. Life becomes a constant power struggle, and *they* must maintain the position of power. By forcing other people to need them and by denying their need of others, shy-aggressive persons remain on the throne.

Herman, an accountant, illustrates this syndrome perfectly. His actions continually frustrate his wife, Shirley, but he is unaware of his own subtle motives. Arriving home from the office, he immediately begins to read the evening paper. Shirley tries to break through the obvious barrier between them by initiating simple conversation, but Herman only grunts in response. After this routine continues for a while, Shirley becomes exasperated and gives up trying to start a conversation. She leaves the room and continues her chores.

Herman complains, "Well, I've tried, but she gets mad and I can't talk with her." In this way he justifies his passivity, blaming his wife and refusing to deal with her desire for even a small show of love and companionship. Herman's way of passive-aggressively avoiding the issue of Shirley's feelings makes him feel superior. He sees in his wife someone out to manipulate him by making him feel needy. And he sees his ultimate task as avoiding manipulation.

When passive-aggressive people believe they are being manipulated, they feel an immense threat to their identity. Sometimes they react by parading a cocky superiority. At other times they become extremely quiet, saying just enough to irritate the other person or cleverly miss the point of a conversation. They tune out criticism against themselves and thus "win" each confrontation. By avoiding their own tender feelings, they maintain their position of power. *But these people are shy only in situations involving their tender feelings. And the sad truth is, they would rather fight than love!*

One example of the shy-aggressive type in the New Testament is found in the young man of Jesus' parable who gladly responded to his father's command to work in the vineyard but never went out to report for duty.

Shy-Terrified

The shy men whose world is most distorted are those who live in constant terror of their own rage and of other people's rage toward them. They withdraw almost totally from society, preferring to live in their own fantasies. They can tolerate little social contact and frequently withdraw physically or mentally. These are *the shy-terrified.*

Their profoundest wish is to be held by a perfect mother or father and cuddled forever. Since every situation falls short of this fantasy, they live in constant rage because their wishes are not being fulfilled. To guard themselves against such terribly unpleasant feelings, they withdraw from people. As a result, they are often known as eccentric, peculiar, reclusive, or, in extreme cases, hermits.

If in social situations their wishes are constantly frustrated, their rage boils to the point that they live in terror of exploding with violent behavior. If they could describe their feelings, they would say, "I could kill everyone in this room!" or, "I could blow up the whole world!" or, "If I had a gun, I'd shoot everyone here!" To avoid such actions, they simply deny their rage and withdraw.

Occasionally shy-terrified men explode in the type of dramatic actions that make banner headlines in the newspapers. The media routinely carry stories of a shy-terrified man who opens fire on innocent victims or who murders parents, neighbors, or perhaps strangers. Usually, however, such persons are able to control their rage.

Most often the shy-terrified man does not recognize his inner rage. Here are some clues:

- The shy-terrified man is afraid of others and usually denies his own rage by assuming that the other person is angry.
- He fantasizes about being comforted, held, and cuddled.
- Sometimes he feels as if other people are likely to do violent harm to him and others.
- He finds himself not being able to pay attention to others, even though he tries, and wants to withdraw from people.

Bob was twenty-nine before he sought help for his shyness. Friends had always excused him: "You know Bob—he's so shy he hardly ever comes to our activities. And when he does, he stays to himself."

Bob would stand in the back of a group rather than sit with the rest. His therapy sessions revealed many and varied fantasies. He particularly relished one in which he bought a gun and shot people at random. His imagination so frightened him that he was ready and eager for therapy.

Today Bob understands why he is shy, and he is able to face his rage and control it. He's dating, joining in group activities, and working his way out of his fantasies.

"I can feel my rage," he said after two and a half years of therapy, "but now I understand it. And since I can see where it's coming from, I seem to have the power to reduce its effect on me."

On August 1, 1966, Charles Joseph Whitman climbed a tower at the University of Texas at Austin and opened fire on citizens below. When his shooting spree ended, sixteen people lay dead and twenty-five wounded. Whitman had been an Eagle Scout, a concert pianist, and a model husband and father. After the tragedy, friends remembered he had told them repeatedly that he was thinking of climbing the tower and shooting people with a deer rifle. At age twenty-five, Charlie Whitman—"the thinker"—could no longer outrun his rage. He performed the unthinkable violence of his imagination, paying for it with his death—and with the death of his wife, who had been his first victim that dreadful afternoon.[3]

There are other tragic examples of such unchecked rage:

A young man eighteen years old strangled a seven-year-old girl in a New York church. He was known to his friends as unemotional and had made plans to become a minister.[4]

In Phoenix, a polite, soft-spoken eleven-year-old boy stabbed his brother thirty-four times.[5]

The shy-terrified usually has had severe disturbances in his early childhood. He needs to seek professional help over a long period to work through his distorted feelings and fears about himself and others.

Shy-Anxious

Handwringing is a typical manifestation of *the shy-anxious person's* problem. Shy-anxious men find it extremely difficult to be involved in prolonged or deep conversations with people. They spend much of their time flitting from one situation to the next.

The shy-anxious man might be a comedian or a good storyteller. Sometimes he can appear to be a bully. He may be a flashy dresser who wears fancy jewelry and drives a flashy car, or has tendencies toward exhibitionism.

In clinical psychology, shy-anxious men are known as *hysterical personalities*—people who are afraid to see themselves as they really are. Many fear being truly male; masculine aggression in sexuality is something they have never accepted in themselves. They have a profound fear that expression of sexuality or aggression is bad and will lead to disapproval by parents. Forever fixed at puberty, they are afraid to move through adolescence and adulthood recognizing that sexual feelings are normal and healthy. They are perpetual junior highers, with all the accompanying exhibitionism, fadism, and rapid fluctuations of emotions. They fear responsibility and commitment.

Shy-anxious men cling to a fantasy of themselves as being perfect, because if they achieve anything less than perfection, they feel worthless. They are unable to accept any middle ground between being totally good or totally bad. They are likely to be labeled "conceited," since sometimes they believe their own myth that they are as perfect as they wish to be.

Shy-anxious men have an abundance of nervous energy. They talk fast, move fast, twitch, and bob their feet. The devout among them often carry a Bible or other symbols of devotion. They constantly seek support for their fantasies about their moral uprightness, and they deny any evidence to the contrary.

Naturally, shy-anxious men can't become involved with people. They fear that others might find some imperfection in them, so they keep running to avoid any hint of lack or fault. "I'm good at things," they say, turning aside from any situation in which they might obviously fail. They sense they are weak and imperfect, but to acknowledge this consciously would crush their fantasies.

Shy-Contented

Not all shy men are dependent, aggressive, terrified, or anxious. Some merely withdraw without suffering the usual telltale emotions. They don't see their shyness as a problem and when called upon to relate to people, they can do so naturally. But they simply prefer activities they can do alone. Their shyness is perfectly acceptable. These are *the shy-contented.*

Shy-aggressive men want to be served as helpless children.

Shy-dependent men compulsively manipulate people.

Shy-terrified men keep a lock on their rage.

Shy-anxious men remain aloof, lest they reveal any weaknesses.

None of the above describes the *shy-contented.* These men function well. They carry on their activities faithfully, sometimes preferring tasks that leaders could not sit still long enough to accomplish. They are not uncomfortable when involved with people, and they don't cause problems for other people. Shyness is only an occasional problem for them; thus, they have no critical need for alteration.

How to Deal with Shyness

Shy behavior is not necessarily pathological. It becomes pathological only when it is accompanied by unpleasant feelings, bad relationships, and harmful behavior.

Shy men in the first four categories have no easy answers or formulas for change. An evangelist's ten easy steps to maturity or keys to better living may be superficial. No, instead the *person* has to change— and he has to trust God for the grace to enable him to change. That's the longest, hardest route to maturity, but it's the only valid one.

We live in a pragmatic society. Our highest praise is reserved for the inventor or the pioneer. The ideal American male is self-made. Unfortunately, we bring this same mind-set to our psychological problems. The way to have a farm is simply to buy ten acres, chop down the trees, and plant corn. The way to solve a problem in marriage is to touch bases one, two, three, and so on.

Yet for some men there are no simple solutions to their very complex problems. The only place to start is commitment to the enduring truth of the Scriptures, giving allegiance to our Creator and Lord who has redeemed us by His blood.

Shyness can be alleviated. And if you are a shy man who is motivated, you can find help. The first step in overcoming shyness is simply to *begin.* Second, determine the type of shyness you possess. Third, talk about the problem. Fourth, probe—look honestly at how you truly feel deep down. Fifth, talk a lot about the feelings you possess. Sixth, be aware of both your tension and feelings of fulfillment. Finally, see yourself as God sees you—as a complete person.

Most men in the Bible are anything but passive. Some rough, crude, unschooled fishermen ran into a certain Man years ago. He put His hand on their shoulders and said, "Follow Me, and I will make you fishers of men." It was their moment of inspiration. When they were discouraged and felt they didn't amount to anything, He told them, "You are the salt of the earth—and the light of the world!" That great inspirer was Jesus Christ. Draw close to Him, men. Catch His spirit and you will never be the same again.

Life is a lively process of becoming. If you haven't added to your interest during the past year; if you are thinking the same thoughts, relating the same personal experiences, having the same predictable reactions—rigor mortis of the personality has set in.
—General Douglas MacArthur[6]

P TO BE REDJUDICED

*Prejudice, n., a vagrant opinion
without visible means of support.*[1]

SEVEN

Look closely into your heart. Do you find any prejudice there? Be honest—you might come to the same conclusion as the cartoon character Pogo, who once observed, "We have met the enemy and he is us." In that deft phrase, artist Walt Kelly described the subject of this chapter. Few men escape that damning sin called prejudice. We are tempted by it in a hundred ways every day: in dealing with our children, in reaching out to neighbors, in hiring, firing, and interacting with the people on our jobs.

Thirty years ago, a white man named John Howard Griffin shaved his head, changed his skin color from white to black with a chemical, and reentered society in the South as an African American. His book, *Black Like Me*, describes the prejudice he encountered in account after bloodcurdling account. At one time he had lived peaceably in the South, moving freely from place to place as he wished. Now he could go nowhere without meeting the ugly face of prejudice.

The preface of the book sums up the theme of this chapter: "The real story is the universal one of men who destroy the souls and bodies of other men, and in the process destroy themselves for reasons neither really understands. It is the story of the persecuted, the defrauded, the feared and detested."[2]

William James addressed the temptation of prejudice in the lectures that make up his book *Pragmatism*, published in 1907. He wrote:

> Our minds thus grow in spots; and like grease spots, the spots spread. But we let them spread as little as possible: we keep unaltered as much of our old knowledge, as many of our old prejudices and beliefs, as we can. We patch and tinker more than we renew. The novelty soaks in; it stains the ancient mass, but it is also tinged by what absorbs it.

To patch and to tinker is not what Christ had in mind when He addressed the temptation of prejudice. Facing the anger and criticism of the Pharisees and scribes, Jesus had to patiently explain to His disciples later, "Are you thus without understanding also? Do you not perceive that whatever enters a man from outside cannot defile him, because it does not enter his heart but his stomach, and is eliminated. . . . What comes out of a man, that defiles a man" (Mark 7:18–20).

The tongue, fed by the reservoir of a prejudiced heart, pours out slander, criticism, pride, envy, foolishness. It turns the poor against the rich, the rich against the poor, Christians against unbelievers, unbelievers against Christians, the educated against the ignorant, the ignorant against the educated. . . . Prejudice is rife in sports, businesses, schools, stores, rural neighborhoods, even the Church. A man must be on guard every day against prejudice—otherwise he'll spend his life with others who concern themselves with the same prejudices when all around him is a desperately needy world.

Prejudice clouds a man's vision and makes his whole body dull and gloomy. But if his eye is clear, Jesus said, your "whole body will be full of light" (Matt. 6:22). A man who sets aside his prejudices will see an entirely new spectrum of light opening up in his life. He will enjoy new ways of doing business, of extending courtesy to others, of enjoying fresh perspectives in daily conversations.

Prejudice in the Ranks

Those of us who served in the military during World War II saw prejudice firsthand when black soldiers were segregated from whites. That began to change, however, when Lieutenant Roger C. "Bill" Terry, a distinguished flyer of the B-24 "Bridge Buster" bombers in Asia, walked into the segregated white officers' club in Seymour, Indiana, on April 5, 1945. This hulking, six-foot, two-inch flying ace of the United States Air Corps was one of 101 black airmen, many of whom had fought valiantly in the air battles over Italy but still were denied the privileges of their fellow white flyers.

For having the audacity to associate with his peers rather than with trainees at the air base as he was told, Lieutenant Terry was court-martialed. Not until forty-seven years later, in 1992, was the court-martial set aside. "It's kind of late now," Bill Terry told me in Inglewood, California, where he lives. "I would like to have had my court-martial removed 47 years ago because I was forced to put it on every job application I've filled out. This disclosure has hurt my employment prospects and career advancement for the past four decades."

"Not Here, You Won't!"

Men are prejudiced not only against other people but even against methods, procedures, inventions, and programs. Some of this kind of prejudice can be downright amusing:

- When chloroform was discovered nearly a century ago, many people in the religious and medical world fought against its use. Chloroform, they reasoned, was a tool of Satan to rob God of the deep earnest cries that should arise to Him in times of suffering.
- Encyclopedias note that serious scientists wagged their heads at the idea of a vehicle traveling on rails at high speeds, such as on a train. Passengers, they said, would die of asphyxiation.
- Eighteen months before the Wright Brothers took flight in their experimental airplane, scientists had convincingly argued that flight by machines that were heavier than air was impractical and insignificant, if not utterly impossible.
- A Munich schoolmaster had this prejudiced view of his ten-year-old student, Albert Einstein: "You will never amount to very much."

Jesus and Prejudice

The One who suffered most from prejudice never mentioned the word. The Lord Jesus Christ was completely free of it. He deliberately traveled through Samaria when Jews of His day would avoid the region by taking the long way around. They hated Samaritans—but Jesus said He was only emulating His heavenly Father. "I speak what I have seen with My Father," He taught (John 8:38). His detractors snapped back, "We were not born of fornication" (verse 41). What did they mean by that? Simply this: *You* were, *you illegitimate impostor!* They said, "Do we not say rightly that You are a Samaritan and have a demon?" (verse 48). The implication wasn't subtle: *You half-breed son of some Roman soldier and a Jew!* Christ was not a Samaritan, and He did not have a demon, but they charged Him with both.

Day after day as He taught, Jesus faced the specter called prejudice. He met it in the synagogues, on the streets, in the people's homes, and eventually as He stood condemned before Pilate, who was full of prejudice, an anti-Semite to the core. But the idea for Jesus' crucifixion came from the religious leaders of the day—the Pharisees, scribes, Sadducees, chief priests, and elders (Matt. 27:1). Their hatred spread to the common people, whose reckless prejudices ran so deep they called down obligations upon even their own children in order to put to death the Savior of the world. Yes, prejudice is passed on from generation to generation. And Pilate knew full well "they had handed Him over because of envy" (Matt. 27:18). You see, the Jews killed by stoning, but the Romans by crucifying; therefore, to hand Jesus the agony of crucifixion, the Jews changed their charge against Him from a claim to be God to a plan to overthrow Caesar's government. The Romans had many gods—what was one more? They didn't care about Jesus' claim to deity. But insurrection—that was a different matter entirely, punishable by crucifixion.

Men who are nourished by hatred have murder in their hearts. Adolph Hitler killed millions of Jews. Joseph Stalin killed even more millions who resisted Communism. And Pol Pot of the Khmer Rouge slaughtered millions of Vietnamese and Cambodians so he could grab power in those Indochinese countries, which had been worn down by decades of war.

Prejudice in Rigid Homes

Many fathers become angry when their children refuse to toe the narrow line of their self-made rules. *Be careful, fathers, not to provoke your children to wrath!* (Eph. 6:4 paraphrase, emphasis mine). A Christian home can be a breeding ground for hypocrisy. If fathers give their children *only* Bible, Bible, Bible, and God, God, God, without any sense or atmosphere of love, compassion, and tenderness, they can expect them to head straight into rebellion.

Children quickly sense hypocritical religion. They can't stand it. Parents have to keep expectations for home life realistic. They can't make *every* activity include a prayer. And they can't give *everything* a spiritual application; the dynamics of family life, both simple and complex, aren't all meant to provide lessons in theology. Most of all, parents can't force children to conform to a pious "Christian" religious front. I have had to painfully sweep up after the shattering fallout of legalism in the homes of several friends, and it is not pleasant by any stretch of the imagination.

Few stories better illustrate hypocrisy than the one told of a ten-year-old Jewish boy in Germany during World War II. He and his parents lived in a Polish village before they were rounded up and sentenced to death by machine-gun fire.

They stood beside each other, naked, waiting for death. But somehow the bullets that killed his parents missed the boy. He fell with his mother and father and other Jews into a ditch, where soldiers covered their bodies with dirt. Somehow, oxygen reached the boy and he was able to breathe until night fell. Then he clawed his way out of his tomb.

In the darkness, the naked boy made his way to the nearest house, that of a Gentile woman, and begged for help. But the woman recognized him as one of the Jews marked for death by the vicious Nazis, and she screamed and ordered him to go away, slamming the door in his face.

At the next house he was turned away again. Doors kept closing in his face. Finally, at one woman's door, something inside the boy caused him to cry out, "Don't you recognize me? I'm the Jesus you say you love." After a silent pause, the woman in the doorway swept the lad into her arms and kissed him. From that day on, members of her family cared for the boy as one of their own.[3]

> Inasmuch as you did it to one of the least of these My brethren, you did it to Me (Matt. 25:40).

Hypocrisy is nothing new. What will people fifty years from now be saying about Christians in our generation?

> *Judge not, that you be not judged. For with the judgment you pronounce you will be judged, and the measure you give will be the measure you get. Why do you see the speck that is in your brother's eye, but do not notice the log that is in your own eye? Or how can you say to your brother, "Let me take the speck out of your eye," when there is the log in your own eye? You hypocrite, first take the log out of your own eye, and then you will see clearly to take the speck out of your brother's eye.*
> *— Matthew 7:1-5 (RSV)*

G TO GIVE UP

———————————

"It's always too soon to quit."
—V. Raymond Edman,
late president of
Wheaton College[1]

EIGHT

E very man has experi-
enced the temptation
to quit an endeavor short of the goal. Some men stop
short because of shyness, others because of anger,
still others because of fear, and many from sheer
frustration. For a lot of men, these temptations lead
to even greater problems and frustrations. S. Truett
Cathy, founder and chairman of the nationwide
chain of restaurants called Chik-fil-A, made this
point the theme of his autobiography, which is
provocatively titled, *It's Easier To Succeed than To Fail.*
If that is so, why doesn't every man succeed? There
are many reasons.

"We're Not Quitting!"

In the November, 1982 issue of *Guideposts* the
story is told of an Oklahoma rancher named Nelson
Pendergrass and his family who made a dramatic
commitment to a sixteen-year-old boy named David
who was in trouble with the law.

"I thought I was the kind of man that could help
him change," Nelson said as he recalled the early

days with David. But instead of responding to the love the Pendergrass family extended, David withdrew. Their relationship became so strained that Nelson came close to admitting he had failed and sending David back to the juvenile court. The decision was painful even to think about. But with each passing day, David's return to the authorities seemed more certain.

Then one day Nelson was injured in an accident on his ranch. He was rushed to the intensive care unit of the local hospital. While recovering from his injuries, a blood clot formed in his veins and entered his heart. In just moments, Nelson Pendergrass was fighting for his life. The stabbing pain became so intense he was tempted to give in to the welcoming arms of death and end it all.

"I gasped for air," he said, "but it hurt too much to breathe. Better to just drift away, I told myself. Away from the fear, from the pain, forever.

"But there was the nurse, her face not six inches from mine. 'Breathe, you've got to breathe,' she said.

"*Leave me alone,* I wanted to scream. *Let me die.* But no, she was still there. 'Breathe,' she demanded, 'breathe . . . breathe . . . breathe . . . breathe. . . .' I was willing to give up, but she was not. Again and again, I fought to take a breath as she called to me." Nelson survived, thanks to that nurse who made him breathe instead of allowing him to give up.

Back home on the ranch, Nelson began to see more clearly his relationship with his unresponsive teenager. It was his turn to stay with David and insist that he "breathe!" One night they experienced their most critical encounter: David had been arrested for stealing a car. Nelson went to face the boy in the police station holding cell. But David's attitude was, "Leave me alone. I don't care anymore." Then Nelson remembered the nurse who wouldn't let him quit breathing.

"David," he said, "as long as you're under my supervision, you're not giving up on life. And I'm not giving up on you either. We're not quitting. You're coming home. And you and I and the Lord are going to get through all of this."

Today David is a loving young husband and father. He was brought to a place of commitment and responsibility by a man who taught him how to "breathe."[2]

Quitting Is Seldom Right

Not long ago, an old friend named John came to see me with a look of urgency on his face. I asked my secretary to hold all calls so I could give him my full attention.

"Ted," John began, "you know about my real estate company."

Indeed I did—and I was pleased to affirm him in its remarkable growth and in the quality of its services. I also knew that John was generous beyond tithes toward his church, including support for a variety of Christian enterprises.

"Well," John continued, "last week a large company offered to buy me out at a good price. They guarantee I will remain as president and that my salary will increase. I can stay in the company and not have all the headaches of owning it."

"What's the problem?" I asked.

"If I sell my company, I'll lose control and won't be able to give to the Lord off the gross earnings."

The more we talked, the more clear it became to my friend that quitting would be the easy way out. It was not what he wanted to do. That afternoon he made a strategic decision not to give up his company. John retained ownership, continued to give generously out of a grateful heart, and enjoyed his work more than ever.

Loser's Limp

I've been an avid sports fan all my life. Every new magazine or book on sports and athletes tempts me with its alluring fare. That allure has more to do with winners, of course. But the fact is that sports has more quitters than conquering heroes, as the pitiless exacters called the stopwatch and the scoreboard separate the best from the "also-rans."

There is a phenomenon in sports called "loser's limp." Any coach will tell you that many young boys suddenly develop a limp at the end of a race as an excuse for not having done better. That "loser's limp" is the badge of quitters.

It keeps men in all areas of society from attaining their goals. A man with this attitude is beaten before the starter's gun fires. He will never reach far above a subsistence level.

"As you can see," he might say, "I am handicapped by—" But most often he has no handicap at all, only an excuse. Helen Keller had several forgivable liabilities—blindness and deafness among them—but she ignored them. Her achievements are remarkable.

If you are tempted to stop short of realizing your life's potential while other men with no greater gifts than yours are building grand careers and serving God effectively, you are losing life's race. Yet there is still time to be counted in. Even if you've lost a few meets, you don't need to stay on the sidelines.

Recorded in my eclectic notebook is this bit of verse written by an unknown author:

> Because we want to be great,
> He became small.
> Because we will not stoop,
> He humbled Himself.
> Because we want to rule,
> He came to serve.

When It's Okay to Quit

"Just Say No" was the phrase coined by First Lady Nancy Reagan several years ago to admonish young people to avoid the scourge of drugs. I like what Peter L. Ream wrote to people who are hooked on alcohol and won't quit because they justify their habit as being a "disease":

Alcoholism is a disease? If so, it is the only disease that is contracted by an act of the will. It is the only disease that requires a license to propagate it. It is the only disease that is bottled and sold. It is the only disease that promotes crime. It is the only disease that is habit-forming. It is the only disease that is spread by advertising. It is the only disease that is given for a Christmas present.[3]

Here is a final word to all quitters from the apostle Paul:

"Be watchful, stand firm in your faith, be courageous, be strong. Let all that you do be done in love."
— *1 Corinthians 16:13–14 (RSV)*

THE INVULNERABLE MAN

_____

"My master trusts me . . . "
—Genesis 39:8 (TLB)

NINE

My father was a lay minister in Cleveland, Ohio, who enjoyed every opportunity to preach. None of his sermons held more fascination for me than his message on that champion of every man who has ever been tempted—Joseph, son of Jacob, who was sold into slavery by jealous brothers and promoted to become the captain of Potiphar's palace guard. Joseph stood up to temptations that varied in type, but not in degree: his challenges were severe.

Egypt was alive with political and social liberation in the time of the pharaohs when Joseph entered the scene. Pharaoh's domain was the gem of the Middle East where commerce flowed freely and where the women of privilege, including Pharaoh's wife, were quite liberated.

The note to remember here is that men are not always the aggressors in the face of temptation. And it is wrong to think that temptation is always in the area of the sensual life. We can be tempted by things as big as a house and as small as a diamond. We can be tempted by titles and status and degrees and leisure. But the issue that snares most men and causes the most far-reaching agony is the undisciplined male drive for sexual conquest. Yielding to it can snatch away a man's family, all he owns, and his future as well, as discussed in Chapter Two. What a terrible price to pay!

The New Kid on the Block

Joseph rode into town on a caravan owned by the Ishmaelite traders who had purchased him from his brothers. The life he had enjoyed in Israel was over forever. He could have been bitter and uncooperative, but something quite different happened. These itinerant merchants probably noticed that their prisoner was not one of their run-of-the mill dust kickers. This bright young lad, with nothing better to do, might have whipped the straggly camels and their riders into a neat and orderly procession as they rode into town. The head Ishmaelite probably figured his slave would bring a good price from the head of the palace guards, so he headed for the Pharaoh's palace.

Potiphar, the captain of Pharaoh's body guards, was a man of wealth and influence. He was always looking for men of strength and intelligence to serve in the court of the king. He must have been at the slave market that day when the Ishmaelites arrived. When he saw Joseph, he bought him and gave him a place of service as one slave among many.

Having no possible way of escape, the young Israelite might have been tempted to turn his back on principle, to do as little as possible, and to live for whatever pleasures he could find in a land from which there was no hope of escaping. But he didn't.

"The LORD was with him," say the Scriptures (Gen. 39:3) and Potiphar took notice that he had purchased a unique fellow. He decided to make this stalwart Hebrew slave his personal aide. Gradually Joseph was promoted up through the ranks until he was in charge of the entire house of Potiphar. The Egyptian, no doubt, was pleased with his choice because the Scriptures say that the Lord began blessing Potiphar for Joseph's sake. "All his household affairs began to run smoothly, his crops flourished and his flocks multiplied" (Gen. 39:5 TLB). Potiphar had not a worry in the world when Joseph was there. The only decisions he had to make were what to eat. Now there's a man who knew how to delegate! But I'm sure he still kept an eye on the books and he could see that because of Joseph, his profits were going through the roof.

It's not a small thing to take people into your home. Sometimes it can be quite disrupting. While serving in the leadership of World Vision International from 1963 to my retirement a quarter of a century later, my wife Dorothy and I had occasion to host hundreds of guests from all parts of the world. Not one took away our privacy; not one made us feel uneasy. This is how Potiphar felt about his Hebrew servant.

Joseph had a servant's heart. He was willing to do the things that made Potiphar look good. It didn't matter to him who got the glory. What a man!

Who Would Know?

A line in the Hebrew text of this story reads, "Joseph was well built and good looking." Here trouble begins. These characteristics of her husband's new slave did not go unnoticed by the lady of the house. She wanted Joseph's good build and good looks for her own.

"It came to pass after these things," says verse 7, "that his master's wife cast longing eyes on Joseph." Her approach was direct: " . . . and she said, 'Lie with me.'"

What man could handle such a direct hit as that? Only men who are on a mission—men like Joseph who do right not only when they are seen but always, knowing that they live *coram deo* (before the face of God and unto His glory).

Every moment of temptation has a lure and a craving to respond to the lure. Joseph was Mrs. Potiphar's lure, his body was her craving, for she desired the pleasurable delight of sharing an intimacy with this servant.

Joseph's response was immediate. First he appealed to her reason: "Having me my master has no concern about anything in the house, and he has put everything that he has in my hand; he is not greater in this house than I am; nor has he kept back anything from me except yourself, because you are his wife" (Gen. 39:8–9 RSV).

But Potiphar's wife kept up her drumbeat of temptation day after day. Still Joseph would not lie with her. He appealed next to her conscience: "How . . . can I do this great wickedness, and sin against God?" (verse 9). It isn't reasonable, he said, to break his trust with his master, but that's reasoning with lust and it cannot be done.

Neither plan worked. "One day, when he went into the house to do his work and none of the men of the house was there in the house, she caught him by his garment, saying, 'Lie with me.' But he left his garment in her hand, and fled and got out of the house" (verses 11–12).

The Indecent Proposal

To accept the woman's proposal would have meant an advancement for Joseph. Potiphar's wife would surely have put in a good word for him in the ear of her husband on Joseph's behalf. He stood to gain immeasurably if he had gone along with her plan.

This woman had no place in her life for God. Joseph, however, had given God first place, and he had no place for disobedience. By refusing to sin he said to the woman, "I cherish my relationship with the Lord. If I involve myself with you in this sin, that will be cut off. I could not endure such a terrible experience. How can I commit this sin before my God?"

Another man might have been impressed by the high rank of the temptress. He might have been flattered by her invitation. It could have led to an easy life and freedom from the drudgery of hard work. Not only was there an opportunity for promotion if he accepted, but there was danger in a refusal because, in the words of William Congreve, "Heaven has no rage like love to hatred turned, Nor hell a fury like a woman scorned."[1]

Humanly speaking, everything was on the side of yielding to the temptation. Joseph had to have been flattered, must have considered what yielding would mean in terms of a promotion, and wanted advancement in the ranks as well as the next fellow.

"When she saw that he had left his garment in her hand, and had fled out of the house, she called to the men of her household and said to them, 'See, he has brought among us a Hebrew to insult us; he came in to me to lie with me and I cried out with a loud voice; and when he heard that I lifted up my voice and cried, he left his garment with me, and fled and got out of the house'" (Gen. 39:13-15 RSV).

Every man reading this will shake his head in admiration at the response of this displaced Hebrew. He was in a foreign country, had no hope ever of seeing his family again, knew his future as a Jew among pagan Egyptians was limited, and yet he was going to do right if the stars fell.

After he ran out of the house you might expect the morning papers to acknowledge this good deed with headlines proclaiming him a hero. Quite the opposite took place. Joseph went to jail.

Gratification Delayed

With pretended rage, Potiphar's wife presented the circumstances as attempted rape. And when her husband heard what she had to say, his anger burned within. He gave the order to put Joseph in jail.

Potiphar was tough. I think he was a man who had ordered many a slave to be killed for disobedience or theft or insubordination. It would have been routine for him to have Joseph taken to the gallows and slain. But instead, he had him put into the jailhouse.

Do you suppose Potiphar had a question about the accuracy of his wife's report? It could be that he didn't believe her and wanted to spare the man he trusted to run the affairs of his house. At any rate, God was watching over Joseph because He was not finished with His work on behalf of His people in Israel.

Confirmed in Holiness

The lessons Joseph's life offer help us make the right choices today:

First, determine in your mind right now that you will not yield to temptation no matter what. If you don't, you'll be flattered to the point of yielding and all will be lost. You'll be no match for temptation's subtle wink.

Second, do not be confused by persuasion. If you can't think clearly now, you won't be able to resist when you're hit with the allure of sin. Joseph could have said all kinds of things if he'd been of a mind to: (1) Potiphar doesn't have what it takes to make love to this beautiful woman as I can, (2) we are perfectly safe; no one ever needs to find out, (3) I'm so terribly violated as a slave and robbed of normal associations. Surely this is God's provision for my needs. . . .

Carry this over to modern times. Can't you hear the hiss of the deceiver in these excuses?

Her husband doesn't love her like I could. . . .

By doing this I could prove that I really care for her. . . .

God knows I'm lonely; He didn't create me to be without this release of my love for another. . . .

My wife cheated on me; I'll get back at her and it will serve her right. . . .

These excuses aren't reserved for the laity. I've traveled the world and talked to stalwart missionaries who are committed to obeying God, but I know they are tempted. When you pray for your missionaries, remember to pray that God will answer their prayers for chastity. This is not a temptation that is unique to modern America.

Joseph was not weak in standing up to his emotions immediately:

- "How then can I . . . sin against God?" (verse 9).
- "He would not listen to her" (verse 10).
- "[He] fled . . . and got out of the house" (verse 12).

Joseph was a practical man. He refused to flirt with temptation. He didn't even consider the misery of his own celibacy. He didn't say to Potiphar's wife, "Meet me in the garden this afternoon. We'll have tea and talk this over."

Joseph contradicts the whine of every man who says he cannot resist. He shows how a man can be pure and well-pleasing to God.

Get hold of your emotions now. Avoid places and books and people that put impure thoughts into your head. Resist the first wee voice of temptation lest it start eroding your senses and cuts a breach wide enough to admit a raging torrent of destruction. Keep in mind: No temptation is strong enough to make you its slave unless you open the door of your mind and heart and let it in.

Repeat with me those penetrating words: "How then can I do this great wickedness, and sin against God?" (Gen. 39:9 RSV). That motto will save you from yourself and give you in return oceans of blessings for a lifetime.

No matter is more urgent. Nothing will affect the ones you love more. Be on guard as if a thief were picking the lock on your front door. Take action as though the roof of your house were on fire. Move as if your child were choking on a piece of meat. Bring that kind of urgency to the matter and you will never fall. Save yourself from the depression that follows the loss of self-confidence brought on by impurity.

Don't be confused if you take a stand and all of Satan's might breaks loose on you. Joseph went to jail, in the providence of God, but the story doesn't end there. The prison experience prepared him to be the means of God's mighty deliverance a few years later for Joseph's family and for an entire nation.

"The LORD was with Joseph and he became a successful man" (Gen. 39:2 RSV). The Lord will be with you, too. Take that as God's promise to you by writing your name in the space provided:

"The Lord was with _____ and he was a successful man."

> *Joseph is a fruitful bough,*
>   *a fruitful bough by a spring;*
>   *his branches run over the wall.*
> *The archers fiercely attacked him,*
>   *shot at him, and harassed him sorely;*
> *yet his bow remained unmoved,*
>   *his arms were made agile*
> *by the hands of the Mighty One of Jacob. . . .*
>   *—Genesis 49:22-24 RSV*

CCRITICAL
CHOICES

"Resting in manhood's pondering repose of If."
—Herman Melville,
Moby Dick [1]

$\mathbf{F}$or all of my adult life, I've carried a pocket memo pad with me everywhere. In it I record not only things to do but stories of people who have faced critical choices and either caught a wave that led to success and joy or sank into the shallows of failure and unhappiness. Many of these stories find their way into my "Eclectic Notebook" for sermon illustrations and editorial anecdotes.

Each one of us is forced to make decisions constantly. Those signposts appear all the time. My old coach never failed to get a warm response when he said, "When you come to a fork in the road *take it!*" Following are stories of men who came to that fork. Some made good decisions, some made bad choices. All of the choices had far-reaching consequences.

The Fatal Gambling Debt

At the start of the second World War, a young man enlisted quickly with enthusiasm to fight in this noble war. However, he soon found himself on a station in a lonely, frozen wasteland peering into a radar scope for most of the day and playing cards at night.

The subtle temptation of gambling began to eat away at the young soldier's heart, promising something for nothing—great riches, really, if only he could master his technique and make the stakes high enough.

The more he played, the deeper he sank into debt and the higher his stack of IOUs rose. Soon it was obvious even to his artificial optimism that he would never in the foreseeable future be able to pay his debt to the soldier with whom he bunked.

Alone on his watch one dark night outside a Quonset hut he observed a shadowy figure entering a sensitive area in which receipts of the PX were stored. Although he couldn't see who it was, he learned the following morning that someone had stolen a large sum of money there. The angry commander announced that he would find out who it was if it took him the rest of the war.

The gambler saw his opportunity. Rising to his feet he said, "Sir, that won't be necessary. I was on duty and I know who entered the PX."

A murmur arose among the soldiers as their compatriot prepared to finger the thief. The gambler turned and pointed to his roommate. "That's the man," he said.

There was no proof whatever that the accused man had entered the PX, but the soldier on watch said he saw the accused (to whom he owed a small fortune) so the suspect was court-martialed. That one decision gave him his freedom from a gambling debt but sent an innocent man to prison.

The soldier, now free from his gambling debts, was unable to forget the injustice. It ruined his later marriage and his business and eventually led to suicide.

The Man Who Said He Would

A young farmer living in the Midwest was in line to inherit a picture-perfect farm with black loam that had grown tall corn and waves of golden grain for several generations of his family. He wanted to marry his high school sweetheart so she could share his life on the family homestead. He would propose, he decided, the day after high school graduation. His dreams were wide and his love strong for the girl with the dancing eyes and bright smile who had stolen his heart.

High school graduation day came and as he had determined, he asked for her hand in marriage. She accepted and a wedding date was set.

The next morning as the girl was traveling to an interview for a job in a nearby town, she was nearly killed in an automobile accident. A drunk driver had crossed over the center line and hit her head-on, emerging from the tangled steel with only bruises.

For five weeks the girl lay in the hospital recuperating from lacerations, broken bones, and a damaged eye whose sight would never be restored. And when she got the news that she would walk with a limp, she feared that the young man who so recently had pledged to be at her side for a lifetime might be unwilling to keep his promise.

She needn't have worried. The young farmer kept his promise, standing strong like the oak trees on the back forty. He made her his wife and they can look back on three decades with their four children and thank God for a commitment to each other that has yielded unspeakable joy.

When It Happened to "Her"

A physician in a small Colorado town wasn't as loyal. He, too, pledged his troth to a beautiful woman who owned a real estate agency. She regularly worked late and arrived home well after dark.

A rapist watched her for a long time until that fateful day when he attacked the woman. Things were never the same again.

The physician took the news hard, forgetting that his wife was the one who was violated. He couldn't look at her without thinking of what had happened to his bride. Intimacy vanished. Quarrels replaced the serenity of their home. The very sight of his wife began to fill the doctor with disgust. He made excuses for working late and canceled their weekly Friday dinners at the country club.

There was no turning back when the physician made his choice. He would leave his wife and put behind him the memory of the rape—the "violation." Her crying and pleading were to no avail. His decision held. The doctor is now in his third marriage and the children of his current "blended" family make no secret of their eagerness to leave home for good as soon as they come of age.

The Detour to Death

In the autumn of 1987, a middle-aged truck driver began to feel aches and pains in his joints. As he herded his eighteen-wheeler down the highways of the land, slicing through cities and rolling across the prairies with his 40,000-pound payload, he found that he was stopping more often at rest stops for quick naps and some exercise.

A physician diagnosed the trouble as early arthritis and prescribed a powerful steroid. It was the kind of medicine that, the trucker learned later, should not be taken for more than six months. This doctor had made the fateful decision to keep the trucker on the drug for more than three years.

The end of the prescription was also the end of the line for the man who wanted nothing more than to stay in the driver's seat and enjoy the romance of the road. But a doctor's inappropriate decision sentenced the trucker to live with bones so brittle that he could break a rib merely by turning over in bed. His active life is over. He spends his days hobbling around in the home of his parents, trying to decide if it would be appropriate to bring suit in a court of law for the mistreatment that has plunged him into despair and shortened his life expectancy.

A Policeman's Close Call

Two San Francisco police officers had worked all night on a case and were exhausted. It was 4 A.M. when the lieutenant approached the driveway of his associate and prepared to say goodnight.

"By the way," the captain said, "you talk a lot about being born again. What does that mean?"

Oh no, the lieutenant thought. *I'm exhausted and it's four in the morning. Couldn't this wait?*

But the curious officer pressed him. In the dim light of the squad car the lieutenant gave his partner God's simple plan of salvation through Jesus Christ and hoped the man would be satisfied, get out of the car, and let him go home to get some sleep. Instead, the captain pressed him further about the eternal matter. He was eager to respond, and the lieutenant almost missed what followed.

"You can give your life to Christ right here in this car," said the lieutenant. "You don't have to wait."

"I'll do it now, then," said the officer.

There in the wee hours of the morning, he made that most critical decision of all—that eternal decision to become a follower of Jesus Christ. Not twenty-four hours later the captain suffered a brain hemorrhage and fell into a coma while on duty. He never regained consciousness and entered the presence of the Lord a week later.

The lieutenant found himself in New Mexico later that year, speaking at a retreat for police officers and their families. At a meal with the parents of an officer the conversation turned to police work in San Francisco. The wife of a policeman spoke of relatives in the city and lamented the tragic death of her nephew through a brain hemorrhage. "The saddest part is," she said, "that nobody in our family can determine whether or not he was a Christian."

The lieutenant asked her to give him the name of the man and a brief description. After she had, he recognized that her nephew was the man he had led to Christ in the squad car that dark morning before sunup. He related to the happy woman what had happened and assured her that she would meet her nephew in heaven.

"I Don't Know Why I Did It!"

A young man in Fresno, California, took summer employment as a truck driver to haul fruit from the San Joaquin Valley to Los Angeles. He and a buddy in another truck repeatedly made the two-hundred-mile run together so that they could help each other in case something mechanical went wrong.

One day at around sundown, one of the young men caught up with the other driver and started to pass him in a tunnel under a railroad track. Just as he was side by side with the other truck and inching ahead slowly, he suddenly braked and dropped in behind. At the other end of the tunnel a heavy caterpillar tractor on a trailer was stalled in the darkness without any lights. Because the passing driver decided for some unknown reason to put on the brakes and get behind the other driver, the man up front who spotted the machinery first was able to swerve into the left lane and avoid hitting the enormous equipment.

As they came out of the tunnel, the first driver pulled over to the side, his hands and legs shaking from the close call. As his buddy drove up behind him he called, "Why did you drop back?"

"I don't know," the second driver said. "Something told me to do it."

"That saved my life," he said. And after some moments of reflection and discussion of the fateful decision they went safely on their way, never to forget the close call in an underpass where a critical decision made all the difference in the life of a truck driver.

He Went Out and It Was Night

An evangelist with an effective ministry for three decades, including two terms as a missionary with his wife and children in the Philippines, found himself involved in sexual misconduct. The misstep took place far from home during extensive itinerant ministries. When the sin was uncovered and confessed, his wife and children were willing to forgive him.

He arrived home in late afternoon to the warm greetings of his family. His wife cooked his favorite food and encouraged him to stay with his family and put the terrible sin behind him.

The evangelist looked at the opportunity squarely but he remembered his new ties whose allure he could not resist. While the food was being put on the table he slipped out a back door with his suits and personal effects and drove away, never to return. The moment of decision came and went, never to return. He has since remarried and has lost the love of the bride of his youth and of his children. He made a critical choice and is suffering today because it was the wrong one.

"Here I Stand!"

Just before the 1949 Los Angeles evangelistic crusade that brought Billy Graham to national prominence, the evangelist was at Forest Home conference grounds in the San Bernardino Mountains about eighty miles east of Los Angeles. There he wrestled with the question of biblical authority. Was the Bible the Word of God? Did it perhaps merely *contain* the Word of God? Was it written by men or God-breathed? Could it be trusted?

In that forest of scraggly pines, cedars, and oaks the young man of thirty years cast aside all doubt; in a critical prayer he determined that he would go to Los Angeles and preach God's Word with authority. And the rest is history.

By Faith He Understood

Two police officers in a New England city were dispatched to apprehend a criminal reportedly cornered in the house of a seaside neighborhood. The two officers had worked together on the same beat for many years and had learned to trust each other. After talking to neighbors they located the house in which the fugitive was hiding. The older officer crept to the back while the younger officer, at a signal, kicked open the front door and yelled for the criminal to freeze.

Just as the young officer spotted the criminal it appeared to the cop he was reaching out for a gun, so he was just about to squeeze the trigger when he heard his fellow officer scream, "Hold your fire!" From the vantage point of the rear entrance, the older policeman could see that the criminal was reaching not for his gun but for a bar of soap that had shot out of his slippery hands when the sudden entrance of the officers had surprised him.

Because the young officer trusted his superior he made the critical decision to hold his fire and the criminal was brought alive to face his accusers.

"The Lord Will Provide"

A Chinese missionary working with his wife among the impoverished community of fellow Chinese in Calcutta, India, often had to make decisions by faith to carry out his programs of mercy and salvation. He and his wife were people of faith who had proven God many times.

One of their proposed projects was a Christian school to help educate children from homes of abject poverty and thus reach into their homes with the gospel. The missionary selected a site and began the process of finding a builder who would erect the Christian school for Calcutta's ragamuffins. The cost would be $15,000 and the money would have to be paid within thirty days.

"You may start pouring cement," the missionary told the building contractor. "God will provide."

Half a world away, the pastor of a large church was embarking on a trip for a missionary medical group on whose board of directors he served. Friends in that church who knew of the Chinese couple serving in Calcutta were exercised to collect funds through a special offering. The church added a small amount, bringing the total to an even $15,000. The pastor tucked the check into his suit pocket, boarded his flight, and was off on his trip that would eventually lead to Calcutta.

When the missionaries met him at the airport in Calcutta he was hospitably cared for in their humble apartment. As they sat talking that night the pastor inquired of their work and was told about the school project recently undertaken by faith.

"How much do you need to start the project?" the traveler asked.

"The builder wants fifteen thousand dollars," the missionaries explained. "We have already begun to build."

"How will you get the money?" the pastor asked.

With a smile of confidence the Chinese man replied, "The Lord always provides the funds for the projects we dedicate to Him."

The pastor reached into his suit pocket, pulled out an envelope, and handed it to the missionaries. "Indeed, the Lord has provided," he said.

Their rejoicing was great that evening. And on the morrow they called the Christians of their congregation together for a special celebration. The critical decision to move ahead by faith for the building had been the right one for Christ and His kingdom and the poor people of Calcutta.

Let God Be God

A Southern California businessman incorporated his building maintenance business in 1970 and sold franchises all over North America. One of them in Toronto started well, then fell on hard times because the franchisee went heavily into debt with one customer who couldn't pay.

The day grew closer when the franchise would either have to stop going into debt by servicing the struggling corporation or continue to provide the service with hopes that the company would be able to pay their entire bill without dragging the service company down with it.

The cut-off day arrived. Early in the morning the Toronto franchisee phoned the head office in California to get his orders. My friend had spent long hours on his knees in prayer. At 8:30 A.M. he was ready with the answer.

"Wait a little longer," he told the franchisee. "Continue to service the account. We're standing behind you in this decision. God will fight for us."

It was the right decision. Not long afterward the delinquent company paid its bill in full and the franchise continued to enjoy solid financial growth.

Choosing Death on an Icy Lake

Each summer, a staff member at Hume Lake Christian Camps sings to the young campers a song he composed on his guitar. The scene is the Roman Empire just before Constantine when the persecution of Christians was outrageously common-place.

In the song, the decree goes out to Rome's military contingents that all soldiers be required to participate in a heathen ceremony praising the emperor. "Forty brave soldiers for Jesus," the song says, stood to reject the emperor's decree, announcing their allegiance instead to their Savior and Lord, Jesus Christ.

Furious, the emperor had his troops build a bath house on a frozen lake to which the forty soldiers would be forced to march naked across the ice. When they arrived at the bath house, the emperor reasoned, all forty would gladly participate in the pagan sacrifice to their earthly ruler and save their skins.

Only one soldier stood guard that night when the "forty brave soldiers for Jesus" took off all their clothing as commanded and started the march across the frozen lake to the bath house. The guard watched in awe as the Christians willingly walked barefoot and naked on the frozen water, singing songs of praise to the Almighty God as they went. At the bath house, they lined up outside, still refusing to enter and participate in the ceremony.

The eyes of the guard at the water's edge were riveted to the men as he marveled at their bravery and noted their resolve. Suddenly he saw one of them break ranks. The traitor turned to enter the bath house to recant his faith, and to obey Caesar. But the heat inside the bath house overcame the shivering body of the traitor and he died instantly.

"Thirty-nine brave soldiers for Jesus" continued to sing songs to God and to worship the Creator as the soldier on the shore watched with increasing awe. Suddenly he laid down his sword, took off his helmet, his uniform, and finally his boots and under garments as well, then he started running across the ice. The thirty-nine soldiers cheered and embraced their brother in Christ and froze to death that night with the hymns of Zion on their lips.

"Forty brave soldiers for Jesus!" the story ends; nothing could change their true hearts. Only for truth would they stand there and die, only for life would they perish. That was a critical choice which they would have eternity to enjoy.

Short of the Goal

The head of a restaurant chain headquartered in Atlanta has taught thirteen-year-old boys in his church for more than three decades. The boys know they have a friend in their teacher and often make bold to ask for favors. Now and then a former student who turns sixteen will come to his teacher for a loan to buy a car.

In one case, the teacher said he would lend a boy $500 if he would listen to a series of six cassettes issued by the church denomination's publishing arm. Near the end of the last tape, the teacher interrupted the tape by inserting his own voice with this message:

"Steve, if you have listened this far, I congratulate you and want to give you the promised loan to help you buy a car. Phone me right away."

Each week the teacher would ask, "Have you listened to those tapes yet?" and Steve would mumble something like, "A little bit," or "Yeah, I listen to one when I get home from school in the evening. . . ."

Finally the day came when the boy announced to his teacher that he had listened to all the tapes.

"Did you hear anything unusual on any of them?" teacher asked.

"No, not really, but I listened to the tapes," Steve insisted.

"Were you awake when you listened to them?" teacher asked.

"Oh, yes sir," Steve replied.

After taking the cassettes back, the teacher told the startled boy about the message he had superimposed on the last tape. "I'm sorry, Steve," he added. "I would have been glad to help you but you didn't keep your promise and you weren't honest with me. I hope this will be a lesson you will remember always."

Little Missteps, Big Pains

Life is full of pesky decisions of seemingly little consequence but which can yield enormous aggravation.

I thought of this when a friend called to say he had worked like a slave revising ten chapters of a book, only to pull the plug on his computer at the end of the day to move a piece of furniture and lose the entire record because it had not been saved.

I think of the friend who changed the oil in his car's engine, then forgot to replace the drain plug and poured five quarts of fresh oil right through the engine, and into the grass. To make matters worse, he then drove off without lubrication and was stopped dead by an engine whose innards had totally congealed, requiring the purchase of a new engine.

Another friend had what he called "the chance of a lifetime" to interview the great literary master

C. S. Lewis. "Now make dead certain," he told his staff, "that I have a tape recorder that's working."

He had a tape recorder that was working, all right, but the staff had forgotten to put in the carrying case a take-up reel for the fresh new tape. In those days before the convenient cassette recorders, a reel could not be used if it had no empty reel to take up the tape which had passed through the recorder head. My friend wrote as fast as he could on his tablet, but there is no record today of the master's voice on tape.

A builder on the central coast of California invited his son to join him in a manufacturing venture. The son did everything right except to have an attorney remove liability through a properly drawn agreement. Because these few lines were missing from the contract, my friend lost his entire retirement of more than $800,000 and had to reopen his construction business and forget plans to enter into a lighter schedule of fewer demands.

A medical worker accidentally increased an immunization dosage for a child to three times what it should be. Her father sat in the doctor's office for a long time, coaxing his daughter to drink what was actually a lethal concoction. When his daughter died, it was almost too much for the father to bear, knowing that he himself had held the poisonous dosage and encouraged his daughter to drink it. He died of a heart attack several months later.

The Sony Corporation laughed when upstart VHS companies challenged its Beta-Max video cassette recorders and players, but in a few years Beta-Max had disappeared from the shelves as VHS systems took over.

Computer corporations smiled when Bill Gates quit Harvard University before graduating to get into his entrepreneurial company he called Microsoft. They aren't laughing now. Today the young man is worth $6.3 billion on paper and his Microsoft's Disk Operating Systems drive nearly 90 percent of the world's personal computers.

Big networks were not worried when Ted Turner bought up small television stations to run movies and then expanded into the news gathering business. Today his Cable News Network (CNN) dominates the world's news gathering industry and is seen and heard by heads of state and commoners around the globe.

Who could have imagined how big Amway (for "The American Way") would eventually become back in 1960 when two men from Michigan started offering biodegradable cleaning materials? Many who made the critical decision to join Amway have made substantial profits.

After the June 17, 1972 Watergate burglary, President Richard M. Nixon called it an issue that would be of interest to people in Washington but that most people in America wouldn't care much about it. Two years later he became the only Commander in Chief in the United States ever to resign.

When You Can't Decide

Not all decisions are clear-cut. The school to attend, the best car for the money, the community to choose when you relocate your family, the employment choices available. . . .

More often than not, however, help is available for the asking. Sometimes it requires many prayers, lots of digging, many letters, phone calls, and personal visits with the people who can help.

An associate working late at work one evening was told by his boss to lie when his wife called and to tell her he was in a meeting. In reality, he was out spying on his wife because he didn't trust her. What should the associate do?

A lawyer took the case of a teenager in New England who was accused of murder. As the lawyer looked into the case, he found that evidence led to the clear conclusion that his own son was the murderer. What should he do?

As we face each critical choice, usually we know what we *should* do. The critical part is having the will to do it. A pastor of mine once said, "Most of my unpleasant work would be unneeded if the people of my congregation just did what they *ought* to do."

Nothing lasts forever. Making the right choices today will yield blessings without number both in our lifetime and in that great day which is still to come.

> *The day of the Lord will come as a thief in the night, in which the heavens will pass away with a great noise, and the elements will melt with fervent heat; both the earth and the works that are in it will be burned up. Therefore, since all these things will be dissolved, what manner of persons ought you to be in holy conduct and godliness?*
>
> *—2 Peter 3:10-11*

WHAT
M CAN ONE
AN DO?

For to me, to live is Christ, and to die is gain.
—Philippians 1:21

ELEVEN

This is the end of the book—but it's not the end of your temptations! Tomorrow, new ones will rise up to taunt you. How will you meet them? You'll probably face not only the temptations listed in this book—to be promiscuous, to chase riches, to seize power, to become angry or passive or prejudiced or a quitter—but indeed, you may also face the temptations to steal, to lie, to ignore a person in need, to brag, to get even, to pad expense accounts, to work too hard, to eat too much, to drive too fast, to watch too much TV, to not spend time with your family, to put off pursuing a dream for fear of failure, to skip prayer, and to read a Scripture verse on the fly at the breakfast table rather than to meditate on a chapter from the Bible.

Even though I am officially retired, I still see a constant stream of men in my office. Their needs haven't changed much since I became an adult male nearly sixty years ago. My prevailing thought as I see them is, what is our life but a record of choices? Civilization is the response of each man to the challenges of his time. Negative or sinful responses slow progress and wreck empires. Positive godly responses foster art, music, industry, and sweeping spiritual revivals.

It's time to start turning things around. Our nation has millions of chronic alcoholics. The rate is staggering. Juvenile crime is increasing. More children are having to grow up in broken or blended households than in traditional families. Child molesting is a national disgrace. Merchandising is riddled with dishonesty. Misrepresentation in advertising is widespread. Television sitcoms reek with immorality. "Marriages" between homosexuals and lesbians are increasing. Art that caters to prurient interests hangs in national galleries, funded by the government.

"I Will"

What difference can one man make? Moses might have asked the same question. He resisted the temptation of luxury in Pharoah's court and delivered the people of God from bondage. Karl Marx wrote *Das Kapital* by candlelight in an obscure apartment and changed the world in forty years. David stood alone in refusing to run his sword through a sleeping Saul, and was later made king of Israel by God.

Yet here are more up-to-date examples that might hit closer to home: The kind word you said to a family on your street did not go unnoticed by the Lord. Your gesture of friendship, your word of witness to a neighbor, your gift of money to a desperate family—all were recorded in eternity.

Just One Kind Word

How many men might have faced their temptations and won if they had had just a little encouragement from you? How many wives would still be with their husbands if they had heard kind words from them? How many children would be happily in subjection to their parents if they had known that Dad was in their corner, no matter what? Men, there are many people around you who long to hear someone say, "I believe in you." Speak up! If you don't, they might never hear the affirmation they need to overcome temptation.

For Want of a Dad

Not long ago, Hallmark Cards of Kansas City assigned several staff members to go into a penitentiary to provide free greeting cards to any inmates who wanted to send one to their mothers. The visitors were amazed by the number of prisoners who lined up to write greetings on a card to send to their mothers. The program was such a success that the company decided to do the same thing a month later to help inmates celebrate Father's Day. To the company's chagrin, however, not one prisoner lined up to send his dad a greeting card.

What do you hear professional football players say most often when they face a TV camera? "Hi, Mom!" You rarely hear them say, "Hi, Dad!" How refreshing it was to see tennis player Pat Cash leap the barrier after a victory at Wimbledon and run into the stands to hug his father.

Join the Revolution

Thirty years ago a book entitled *The Feminine Mystique*, written by Betty Friedan, launched a phenomenon called "the women's movement." It drew under its banner women who believed that their rights, privileges, and even identities had been taken from them by perfidious males.

Today it is men who are taking stock of their values, struggling with feelings of insecurity, looking for ways to cope rather than to anesthetize their pain with drugs, sex, sports, and materialism. Yes, the "men's movement" is upon us. Books, magazine articles, television talk shows, and radio commentaries are attempting to explain what's wrong with men.

It is time to *think of our destiny*, men. We don't have to be victims of our glands. We are not automatons or victims. We are free to make choices, whether noble or ignoble. To live for money, power, or pleasure is to die one day and leave it all behind. Indeed, to live for anything except Christ will mean reaching the end haunted by guilt and despair to match that of Shakespeare's Macbeth:

> Life's but a walking shadow, a poor player
> That struts and frets his hour upon the stage,
> And then is heard no more; it is a tale
> Told by an idiot, full of sound and fury,
> Signifying nothing.

I have known men of substance, men who have "arrived," prominent men, rich men, handsome men—guys who have tasted, chewed, and digested all that this world has to offer. Yet any man who has all these credits in his life, but does not have Jesus Christ, is destined to be empty and shallow. Something remains missing. Jesus said: "If anyone does not abide in Me, he is cast out as a branch and is withered; . . . If you abide in Me, and My words abide in you, you will ask what you desire, and it shall be done for you" (John 15:6-7).

I say to you now what I said to my dinner companion at the beginning of this book: Whatever your temptation is, whatever your special trial might be—why don't you turn it over to God? When you do, your circle of influence will widen as God, through you, touches the lives of other men. And they in turn will make real to others the faith that has been delivered to the saints once for all.

Men, take the eternal view. Do not abdicate your responsibilities in the home. Do not allow promiscuity to tarnish your witness. Avoid the mad pursuit of riches and of power. Be angry and yet do not sin. Root out from your life passivity, prejudice, and the temptation to quit before your work is completed.

You are only one man, *but you are a man*. Christ is the Lord—your choices are clear. So, for as long as you live, pray every day:

Dear God:
Fit me with the armor of God so that I will make right choices today. Deliver me from temptation and sin, and from all error and omission in every association. Make me to be all that You created me to be through Jesus Christ my Lord. Amen.

CHAPTER ONE
To Abdicate

1. Describe a "stouthearted man" you've known, jotting down the key qualities you've admired.
2. Identify one to three areas that you know are sources of temptation for you. Write them down, since recognition of sources of temptation is the first step in avoiding them.
3. Analysts of the 1980s are identifying the excesses of that decade as the reason for the breakdown of ethical behavior. How does a period of prosperity affect our attitudes and behavior as men?
4. Read Matthew 4:1–11 and identify the three defensive measures Jesus took to defuse temptation.
5. What role do expectations of today's American male have in heightening temptation? Page 6.
6. What may be the reasons there is so little difference between a Christian and non-Christian in terms of ethical behavior? Pages 9 and 10.
7. What three steps does Charles Swindoll recommend in battling temptation? Page 11.

CHAPTER TWO
To Be Promiscuous

1. What evidence do the authors present for the pervasiveness of sexual sin among Christian leaders? Do you consider this failure to remain

sexually above reproach a contemporary phenomenon, or are we merely better at identifying and reporting the problem?

2. What are the ramifications of this "Corinthian" symptom in our churches, according to Dr. R. Kent Hughes?

3. Can you identify the steps down the slippery slope of lust in the example of the pastor that starts on page 18? Which step(s) down have you taken—and what is your rationalization?

4. Based on the experience of that pastor, why is it worthwhile getting back on "terra firma" with God, of opting for purity despite failure?

5. Why is a dysfunctional relationship with one's mother so destructive of healthy relationships with the opposite sex?

6. If you were to look back on your marriage, would you label your view of it as a photograph or as a painting? What effect has your view had on your marriage?

7. What are the greatest sources of temptation in your environment? For the fireman it was the easy availability of pornographic materials and videos on the job. That may not be true for you, but every man has a specific situation providing opportunity for lust to grow and be addictive. What steps can you take to reduce temptation?

CHAPTER THREE
To Chase Riches

1. How may the lure of money, or financial gain, subtly enter into our major decisions, like new job opportunities?

2. Though not mentioned by the authors, what may have made the situation of the lawyer who moved to California extremely difficult, since he had a wife and family? Some of our

most difficult decisions ethically can be greatly influenced by the attitudes of spouse or children, who may not emotionally feel/see the ethical dilemma—but do feel the financial impact keenly.

3. Consider the example of the insurance agent in New Mexico. Does God always quickly reward taking an ethical stand, or are you aware of a person who suffered significantly because of taking a stand? Or is taking the stand against unethical behavior its own reward?

4. In the example of the sales representative who entered into a partnership with a dealer, the partner recommended actions that helped reduce federal taxes. What actions have you taken, though they may be illegal, to reduce or avoid taxes?

5. The missionary in Italy discovered that the things he was doing were not pleasing to the Lord and took deliberate steps to correct his "stealing." What behavior or action has the Lord brought to your mind that is unethical or morally not right?

6. Could the Lord today be withholding blessing from a whole congregation, as He did with Israel at Ai, because of the sin of greed? Or does the Lord not operate by that principle anymore? Examine Ephesians 4:20–32 in the light of the apostle Paul's teaching on the body in that chapter.

7. Can you illustrate Luke 7:38 from your own life, or that of a friend?

8. How can we spend money in ways that will accumulate treasure in heaven rather than on earth? If you have not already done so, select a program, a ministry, an outreach, that you could support above your tithe to your church, and thus experience the blessings of sacrificial giving.

CHAPTER FOUR
To Seize Power

1. What is the difference between the "Gentile rulers" and the disciple of Christ, according to Mark 10:42–44?
2. In what areas of your life do you feel as though you have power—and in what areas do you feel powerless?
3. How can we get more power and have less anger?
4. If you are married, what is one of the areas in your marriage relationship that could be labeled as a "power struggle"? How can men back off and become more of a servant without becoming a Caspar Milquetoast?
5. In what ways have you seen men attempt to exert power, whether at the office or in the church?
6. What is the difference between power and authority? Page 61.
7. Why do men often have real difficulty feeling adequate in comparison to what they perceive their wives' expectations to be?
8. What was the secret to the author's neighbor gaining power in the family? Can you apply this to your office and home situation?

CHAPTER FIVE
To Be Angry

1. Highlight the sentence in the first few paragraphs that best describes the anger you are experiencing.
2. More and more men are expressing their feelings of weakness by resorting to acts of angry violence. Most of these acts occur in the home. If you really want to deal with anger, ask your associates, your wife, your children,

how they would rate you in respect to anger
and angry outbursts on the following scale
(with 5 being most desirable):

a. Is always in control of his emotional
reactions to negative situations.
___0 ___1 ___2 ___3___4___5

b. Flares up quickly, but the anger dies down
quickly, and he frequently apologizes for his
anger.
___0 ___1 ___2 ___3___4___5

c. Does a slow burn when crossed or fails to
achieve his goal, erupting suddenly in a
seemingly unrelated situation.
___0 ___1 ___2 ___3___4___5

d. When crossed or rejected explodes quickly
and violently, arousing fear among those
around him.
___0 ___1 ___2 ___3___4___5

e. Does not seem to get angry often, but will
hold a grudge for a long time.
___0 ___1 ___2 ___3___4___5

3. What is a symptom of the man who must be
   "perfect" in everything he does?
4. In the example of a bank overcharging
   customers, which of the four responses most
   closely matches yours? What does this imply
   for how you handle anger?
5. What would be an example of righteous
   indignation?
6. What may be the reason when someone lashes
   out at a subordinate, a supervisor, or his
   family?
7. Do you consider angry men responsible for
   their behavior? Why or why not?
8. Based on the experience of the pastor in the
   restaurant, what is the most likely response
   when we confess our explosions of anger as
   sin and ask for forgiveness?

9. What steps can you take to deal with anger in your life? You may need the help of a counselor, a pastor, or a friend willing to hold you accountable.

CHAPTER SIX
To Be Passive

1. What are the effects of isolation, competition, and loneliness on modern man?
2. Did you identify yourself in the descriptions of one of the five kinds of shy men? If so, write out some of the symptoms—and if married, let your wife see them so she can help you come to terms with how you come across to others. We recognize that may be very threatening to you, but facing reality can lead to genuine progress.
3. What steps do you need to take to mature and be released from the negative features of your personality? Examine the eight steps for possibility thinking, and focus on one at a time.

CHAPTER SEVEN
To Be Prejudiced

1. As you read this chapter, what area(s) of prejudice in your life was brought to your attention? Be totally honest with yourself, letting the Holy Spirit surface what you may not even have been fully aware of.
2. Rate yourself on the following Prejudice Scale:
   ___Yes ___No 1. During the past year I have helped reach out to the homeless by volunteering time or donating money or food.
   ___Yes ___No 2. During the past year I have shared my faith with someone not my race or color.

___Yes ___No 3. During the past year I have interacted with a someone from a race other than my own.

___Yes ___No 4. I live in a community with no ethnic diversity.

___Yes ___No 5. I would rather move out than to have someone from another race move next door.

___Yes ___No 6. I often complain that the rich are not paying their fair share of taxes.

___Yes ___No 7. I believe homosexuals who are not acting out and have put their faith in Christ should receive acceptance in the church as active members.

___Yes ___No 8. If I went into a restaurant and there was only one seat available, and that was opposite a person of another race, I would join him.

___Yes ___No 9. If a woman was appointed our church choir leader, I would stop singing in the choir.

___Yes ___No 10. If I was invited to a club that excluded Jews, I would not join it.

If you answered six with "Yes" and four with "No" you are truly manifesting the Spirit of Christ in your relationships. If you had fewer "Yes" answers and more "No" answers, then maybe you need to examine the attitude of Jesus Christ toward others.

3. Why is prejudice so difficult to overcome as an adult?

4. How did Jesus respond to prejudice against Him?

5. Translate the example of the Jewish boy in Poland into contemporary suburban life. If a disheveled, nearly naked, small, black, Hispanic, or Oriental child knocked on your door after darkness set in and asked for help, would you open your home to him in the

name of Jesus? Or would you consider the situation a "set up" and quickly close the door?

6. Since Jesus had more to say about helping the poor than preaching the gospel, what proportion of your efforts, your church's efforts, involve evangelistic, loving outreach to the poor and homeless, those of other ethnic backgrounds *in your community?*

CHAPTER EIGHT
To Give Up

1. What relationship in your life might be compared to that of Nelson Pendergrass and David? Your relationship to your wife? A son or daughter? An employee battling alcohol or drugs (or both)? Ask yourself:
   a. Why am I tempted to give up?
   b. What are the benefits of giving up?
   c. What are the benefits of not giving up?
   d. If He were here, would Jesus give up?
   e. From where do I draw the resources to "never give up"?
2. If you have faced an "I want to give up" situation and stuck with it until you saw positive results, review why you eventually experienced positive results. Thank God for His faithfulness in your life.
3. If you are a father, what steps can you take to stop a child that is consistently starting things and giving up too soon?
4. What is the "loser's limp" you use as your excuse for not succeeding at your job, in your church, as a husband and parent?
5. What were the benefits gained by the Youth for Christ staff member who turned down the lucrative offer from an international company?

CHAPTER NINE
The Invulnerable Man

1. Have you, like Joseph, faced severe temptations? What have you learned about God—and yourself—as you faced them? Has 1 Cor. 10:13 been proved true in your situation?
2. What is a "small temptation" that nags at you and refuses to be quelled?
3. What things do you do that make your boss look good? Are you able to "share the glory" for a job well done as Joseph did for Potiphar?
4. How might a man handle a "direct hit" such as the one Potiphar's wife made on Joseph? Why is it impossible to "reason with lust"?
5. Do you tend to do rightly only when others see you, or do you live consciously *coram deo* (see p. 126)?
6. Have you ever faced compromise as a means to promotion? If you passed up the temptation, what gave you strength to do it? If you didn't, what did you learn from the experience?
7. What daily step can you take to be "confirmed in holiness"? How will this help you to be a man who is like Joseph "invulnerable to sin"?

CHAPTER TEN
Critical Choices

1. Think of a fork in the road you've faced. How did you decide which way to go? Was it the right choice? What have you learned about seeking God's will at those signposts?
2. Are you currently seeking "something for nothing," much like the gambler? Be honest—do you see ways your interests are becoming obsessions? What can you do to get control before it costs more than you can afford to lose?

3. Do you know a man who has "stood strong like an oak tree" during moments of crisis? What do you admire most about him?

4. Have you ever missed an opportunity to share the gospel because you were "just too tired"?

5. Has trust in a superior ever saved you from a critical misstep? Are you a trustworthy superior?

6. Given the opportunity, could you be a "brave soldier for Jesus"? If you don't think so, what areas do you need to work on in your spiritual life (how can you grow in bravery)?

CHAPTER ELEVEN
What Can One Man Do?

1. What is the one area that God has laid on your heart as the place or program in which you can make a difference?

2. What kind of effort will it take to make that difference? Write it down as a commitment to making a difference—and begin doing what it will take today.

3. Maybe it is "gut check time" for you as a person, as a husband, as a father, at work, in your church. Describe the situation. Then find a person who can become your "coach" and point you to the goal.

4. Wives tell us that words of encouragement are all too few. How can you encourage your wife today? Be specific about what she means to you, or something she is doing for you.

5. If your son were offered a greeting card to write his dad, would he accept it? If you are concerned that he might not, there is still time to build a new relationship with him.

6. Who in your circle of male contacts needs the word of encouragement you can give? Take time this week to make contact and lift that

person's spirit as you listen, encourage, and pray with him.

7. All of us struggle with temptation of one kind or another. What, according to this chapter, is the most important truth to remember and act upon?

Chapter One
To Abdicate

1. Robert Henrick, (1591-1674), "Temptations" (1648).
2. Lord Byron, "On My Thirty-sixth Year" (1824).
3. David Nyhan, "Wanted: Some Stouthearted Men," *Boston Globe,* 7 May 1988, 87.
4. R. Kent Hughes, *Disciplines of a Godly Man* (Wheaton, Ill.: Crossway Books, 1991), 119.
5. James Patterson and Peter Kim, *The Day America Told the Truth* (New York: Prentice Hall, 1991), 3. Used by permission of the publisher, Prentice-Hall Press/a Division of Simon & Schuster, New York.
6. Ibid., 25.
7. Dietrich Bonhoeffer, *Creation and Fall / Temptation* (New York: Macmillan, 1959), 118.
8. Patterson and Kim, *The Day America Told the Truth,* 157.
9. Doug Sherman and William Hendricks, *Keeping Your Ethical Edge Sharp* (Colorado Springs: NavPress, 1990), 25.
10. Patterson and Kim, *The Day America Told the Truth,* 125.
11. Charles R. Swindoll, "Christ at the Crossroads of Temptation," sermon preached at First Evangelical Free Church, Fullerton, California, 4 March 1990. Used by permission.
12. Walter Wangerin, Jr., *Reliving the Passion* (Grand Rapids: Zondervan Publishing House).

Chapter Two
To Be Promiscuous

1. Frederick Buechner, *Godric* (San Francisco: Harper San Francisco, 1983).
2. Robert H. Bork, *The Tempting of America* (New York: The Free Press, 1990), 212.
3. "How Common Is Pastoral Indiscretion?" *Leadership,* Winter 1988, 12.
4. R. Kent Hughes, *Disciplines of a Godly Man* (Wheaton, Ill.: Crossway Books, 1991), 23.
5. Ibid., 24.
6. A. W. Tozer, *That Incredible Christian* (Harrisburg, Pa.: Christian Publications, 1986), 14.
7. Anonymous, "The War Within," *Leadership*, Fall 1982, 35-36.
8. Ibid., 42.
9. Ibid., 48.
10. Stephen Strang, "Enough Is Enough," *Charisma*, June 1992, 10.
11. Anonymous, "The War Within Continues," *Leadership*, Winter 1988, 28.
12. Mark Twain, *Puddinhead Wilson's New Calendar*, quoted in *Bartlett's Familiar Quotations*, John Bartlett, (Boston: Little, Brown and Co., 1980), 625.
13. Anonymous, "The War Within Continues," *Leadership*, Winter 1988, 29.
14. Edwin Louis Cole, *On Becoming a Real Man* (Nashville: Thomas Nelson Publishers, 1992), 113.
15. Ibid., 113.
16. Anonymous, "The War Within Continues," *Leadership*, Winter 1988, 24.
17. Ibid., 24.
18. Keith Miller, *Habitations of Dragons* (Irving, Tex.: Word Books, 1970).

Chapter Three
To Chase Riches

1. Tennessee Williams, *The Glass Menagerie*, sc.vii (1945), in *Bartlett's Familiar Quotations*, John Bartlett (Boston: Little, Brown and Co., 1980), 887.
2. James Patterson and Peter Kim, *The Day America Told the Truth* (New York: Prentice Hall, 1991), 3. Used by permission of the publisher, Prentice Hall Press/a Division of Simon & Schuster, New York.
3. George S. Clason, *The Richest Man in Babylon* (New York: Signet, 1988), 28-29.
4. James C. Dobson, *Straight Talk* (Irving, TX: Word Books, 1991), 170.

Chapter Four
To Seize Power

1. Warren Farrell, Ph.D., *Why Men Are the Way They Are* (New York: Berkley Books, 1986), 9.
2. Fremont E. Kast and James E. Rosenzweig, *Organizations and Management* (New York: McGraw-Hill, 1974), 333.
3. John Emerich Edward Dalberg Lord Acton. Letter to Bishop Mandell Creighton [24 April, 1881], quoted in *Bartlett's Familiar Quotations*, John Bartlett (Boston: Little, Brown and Co., 1980), 615.
4. Richard Foster, *Money, Sex, and Power* (San Francisco: Harper & Row, 1985), 178-179.
5. Charles Colson, *Who Speaks for God?* (Westchester, Ill.: Crossway Books, 1985), 40.
6. John W. Gardner, *The Nature of Leadership* (Washington, D.C.: Independent Sector, 1986), 7.
7. C. S. Lewis, *Mere Christianity* (New York: Macmillan, 1958).

8. Quoted in Marine Corps recruitment manual, El Toro, Calif., 1990.

Chapter Five
To Be Angry

1. J. K. Hoyt, *Cyclopedia of Practical Quotations* (New York: Funk and Wagnalls, 1896), 677.
2. Norman B. Roher and Philip S. Sutherland, *Facing Anger* (Minneapolis, Minn.: Augsburg Fortress, 1981), 8 from J. K. Hoyt *Cyclopedia of Practical Quotations* (New York: Funk and Wagnalls, 1896), 17.
3. Ibid., 8.
4. James Patterson and Peter Kim, *The Day America Told the Truth* (New York: Prentice Hall, 1991), 3. Used by permission of the publisher, Prentice Hall Press/a Division of Simon & Schuster, New York.
5. Leonard E. LeSourd, *Strong Men, Weak Men* (Old Tappan, N.J.: Chosen Books, 1990), 126.
6. David Stoop and Stephen Arterburn, *The Angry Man* (Irving, TX: Word Books, 1991), 45.
7. Ron R. Lee, "After the Revolution," *Marriage Partnership,* Spring 1988, 53.
8. Thomas DeQuincey, quoted in *Bartlett's Familiar Quotations*, John Bartlett (Boston: Little, Brown and Co., 1980), 454.

Chapter Six
To Be Passive

1. Philip G. Zimbardo, *Shyness* (Reading, Mass.: Addison-Wesley Pub. Co., 1977), 5.
2. Norman B. Rohrer and Philip S. Sutherland, *Why Am I Shy?* (Minneapolis, Minn.: Augsberg-Fortress, 1978) 26.
3. Aug. 2, 1966, Long Beach, Calif., *Press-Telegram Newspaper.*

4. Rohrer and Sutherland, *Why Am I Shy?*, 48.
5. Ibid.
6. Marine recruitment bulletin, El Toro, Calif., 1990.

Chapter Seven
To Be Prejudiced

1. Ambrose Bierce, *The Devil's Dictionary*, quoted in *Bartlett's Familiar Quotations*, John Bartlett (Boston: Little, Brown and Co., 1980) 647.
2. John Howard Griffin, *Black Like Me* (New York: NAL-Dutton, 1962).
3. Illustration used Dr. Ben Haden, TV speaker for program "Change Points Television," Chattanooga, Tenn.

Chapter Eight
To Give Up

1. V. Raymond Edman, chapel message given at Wheaton College, Wheaton, Illinois, February 1950.
2. Reprinted with permission from *Guideposts* Magazine. Copyright © 1982 by Guideposts Associates, Inc., Carmel, New York 10512.
3. J. Allan Petersen, ed., *For Men Only* (Wheaton, Ill.: Tyndale House Publishers, 1973), 45.

Chapter Nine
The Invulnerable Man

1. William Congreve, *The Mourning Bride* (1697), act 1, sc. 1, sentiments expressed also by Colley Cibber in *Love's Last Shift* (1696), act 4, both contained in *Bartlett's Familiar Quotations*, John Bartlett (Boston: Little, Brown and Co., 1980), 324.

Chapter Ten
Critical Choices

1. Herman Melville, *Moby Dick, Bartlett's Familiar Quotations*, John Bartlett (Boston: Little, Brown and Co., 1980), 571.